ACTION
MANAGEMENT

Practical Strategies for Making Your Corporate Transformation a Success

ACTION MANAGEMENT

Stephen Redwood
Charles Goldwasser
Simon Street

PRICEWATERHOUSE COOPERS

John Wiley & Sons, Inc.
New York ◆ Chichester ◆ Weinheim ◆ Brisbane ◆ Singapore ◆ Toronto

Printed in the United States of America.

10 9 8 7 6 5 4 3 2 1

CONTENTS

FOREWORD

Here is a book that introduces a new way of managing in the post-change era. The authors call it *action management,* and it is just that.

By definition, *action management* is any project or initiative aimed at improving business performance. A change-management program is an action; so is a merger or acquisition, and so is the installation of enterprise resource planning (ERP) software.

Drawing on their experience and that of hundreds of managers around the world, Stephen Redwood, Simon Street, and Charles Goldwasser pinpoint the 10 challenges managers must meet and master to complete a business action. They also provide a blueprint for constructing your own successful action program.

Whatever move you are envisioning that affects operations, functions, or departments in a major way—Redwood, Street, and Goldwasser take you from the planning stages on through to design and implementation.

I urge you to read what this knowledgeable trio from PricewaterhouseCoopers has to say. Then apply their on-the-mark observations and advice to produce results for your own organization. You will be glad you did.

—Richard Pascale

BUSINESS IS ACTION

An action is any project or initiative aimed at improving business performance. A change program is an action. So is reengineering. And so is a merger or acquisition. Understanding what an action is—that's easy. Knowing how to manage it is what bedevils managers from one end of the business world to the other.

1

THE CALL TO ACTION MANAGEMENT

Action is a necessity—to stand in place is to fall behind.
Embrace action. Your business life is on the line.

Mark your calendar for October 26, 2028. On that day, Asteroid 1997 XF11 is scheduled to pass close to Earth, perhaps as close as 180,000 miles, the distance between us and the moon. Should the asteroid collide with our planet, life as we know it would end.

Astronomers at the International Astronomical Union in Paris predicted the close pass in March 1998. But then scientists at the National Aeronautics and Space Administration (NASA) in Houston, Texas, weighed in with a less menacing scenario. Asteroid XF11, they pointed out, orbits our sun, some 140 million miles away. And although it crosses Earth's path every 632 days, it poses no threat. In fact, the NASA scientists calculate that at our closest brush with the asteroid in the next 100 years, it will still be some 600,000 miles away.

That's good news for a planet that has already had some notable encounters with objects from outer space. One theory attributes the extinction of the dinosaurs, for example, to climatic changes that occurred after an asteroid five times the size of XF11 smashed into the Yucatan Peninsula in southeastern Mexico.

Now, NASA scientists are designing a spacecraft that will orbit and track another asteroid, Eros 433. At a cost of $150 million, the Near-Earth Asteroid Rendezvous (NEAR) mission will give scientists a good chance to study such agents of potential change but probably little chance to affect them.

Should an asteroid like XF11 or Eros come too close, perhaps the best we could hope for is a real-life imitation of the Bruce Willis movie, *Armageddon.* In that film, a band of renegade astronauts install a nuclear device on an approaching asteroid. When the device is detonated, the asteroid's course, and the course of history, are changed.

And what, you may ask, has any of this to do with business? Answer: The threat of asteroid collision and the corresponding effort to control it illustrate a basic tenet of this book, a tenet that is as applicable to business as it is to astronomy.

At its core is the stark distinction between a *change,* as represented by the oncoming asteroid, and an *action,* as represented by the NEAR mission and the Willis gang. We argue that business action differs from business change, that a business action can be consciously controlled while business change is largely beyond control.

In recent years, dozens of books have promised to help us control business change by managing it through process reengineering and other techniques. The often ingenious ideas have spawned a record number of corporate makeovers, but with uneven results.

Why? The approaches are based on faulty assumptions. Despite all the talk of change management, we somehow failed to recognize that we can't, in any meaningful sense, manage change. We can only manage our actions—hence, *action management.*

Consider a sloop skimming across a lake, the wind filling its sails. Suddenly, the wind shifts. The captain can't control the change of the wind any more than scientists can control the orbits of asteroids. What he can do, though, is take action to control the boat, turning it to recapture the wind in its sails. The captain is managing his actions to cope with change.

In substance, that is the mission of this book: to help you act, to help you navigate in a business world lashed by ever-shifting winds.

What do we mean by *action*?

The dictionary defines it as "the consciously willed process of acting; an exertion of power or force, as in 'the action of wind upon a sail.' " We define it as *any consciously directed project or initiative that seeks to improve business performance*—meaning the performance of people working alone, in teams, or as an entire organization.

A business or culture change program is, in our parlance, an action. So is the reengineering of business processes. And so are mergers and acquisitions; the restructuring of operations, business units, functions, or departments; and the installation of data management, knowledge management, or enterprise resource planning (ERP) software.

An action, we believe, passes through five predictable stages. It begins with *initiation* (stage one) and progresses through *analysis* (stage two), *definition* (stage three), *transition* (stage four), and *improvement* (stage five).

The initiation stage is when managers take stock and decide to launch the action. In the analysis stage, they study the organization's current situation and look for opportunities to make improvements. During definition, they envision where the organization needs to be and specify the details required to get there. When the action is in transition—a stage that may take years to complete—managers move the organization from where it is to where it must be. And, finally, in the improvement stage, the action is consolidated and expanded through continuous improvement.

Understanding business action and its predictable stages—that's the easy part. Knowing how to manage it—how to design it, direct it, and implement it skillfully and effectively in the face of great pressure—that is the problem that bedevils managers from one end of the business world to the other.

It also is the focus of this book. And skillfully manage you must if you are to succeed today, for the ability to navigate through the choppy waters of business change is critical to sustaining competitive advantage.

The people who manage action may be senior executives. They may also come from the ranks of middle management or from the front line. An action can originate at any place in the organization, too. But wherever it starts, its managers must share a can-do attitude about tackling challenges head-on, especially those that seem daunting to just about everybody else.

The balance of this chapter gives you a preview of our ideas, but first we want to make one thing perfectly clear: From the book's inception, we were determined that it would address the everyday problems that managers face.

So, in 1996, we at PricewaterhouseCoopers set about conducting an in-depth survey of more than 500 multinational businesses in 14 countries in Europe, North America, Asia, and Australia. Industries ranging from high technology and financial services to petroleum and health care were included, as were companies as varied as British Airways Engineering, Braun (the German subsidiary of The Gillette Company), Kawasaki Heavy Industries, Ltd., and Carlton & United Breweries Ltd.

We undertook our Global Action Survey because we wanted to know what barriers managers encounter when they take business action and how they overcome those barriers. We also wanted to know what lessons might be derived from their shared successes—and failures.

Our research led us to identify 10 chief challenges that managers face in taking action. We define those challenges as: *plan, allocate, lead, strengthen, mobilize, clarify, cultivate, integrate, wire,* and *reenergize.* Each challenge aims to address and eliminate a specific barrier to effective action. Let's examine each in turn.

CHALLENGE: **Plan for Action**

An action without a plan is doomed to fail. Thirty-one percent of our Global Action Survey respondents indicated as much. One of them even called planning "*the* most critical part" of his action. So, in Chapter 3, we detail—and illustrate with examples from Adaptec, Inc., Braun, and Carlton & United—the three activities of action planning: setting strategy, making a plan, and managing the action.

CHALLENGE: **Allocate for Action**

Effective action requires the right dedicated resources, said 48 percent of our respondents. That's why we recommend techniques in Chapter 4 that you can use to secure the resources required to make your action work. We illustrate those techniques with case studies of actions undertaken by Adaptec and Bristol-Myers Squibb Company, among others.

CHALLENGE: **Lead for Action**

Action leaders need a specific set of skills, according to some 43 percent of those participating in our survey. So, in Chapter 5 we show you how to help your leaders develop the required skills. We also show how action leadership works at Carlton & United, The Neiman Marcus Group Inc., and others.

CHALLENGE: **Strengthen for Action**

Actions don't stand a chance without middle management support, concluded 38 percent of our respondents. In Chapter 6, therefore, we detail how you can identify and condition the best middle managers, and we provide two cases in point—consumer-products manufacturer Braun and Iberdrola, the Spanish electric utility.

CHALLENGE: Mobilize for Action

Actions need enthusiastic, motivated people. Some 33 percent of the Global Action Survey respondents told us that, and we concur. That's why in Chapter 7, drawing on the examples of Carlton & United and Iberdrola, we suggest ways that you can get and keep your workforce moving.

CHALLENGE: Clarify for Action

If people don't know why they should act, they won't—so said 35 percent of our survey participants. In Chapter 8 we reveal—and illustrate with cases from Adaptec, Barclaycard (a division of Barclays Bank PLC), and Shell Information Services (a Shell Group Company)—how to construct a communications program that does more than simply sell an action: It sustains one.

CHALLENGE: Cultivate for Action

Effective human resources are the linchpin of effective business action, according to some 33 percent of our respondents. So, in Chapter 9, we show you how to support your action's prime asset—with the help of your human-resources professionals—from beginning to end. We also show you how businesses like Neiman Marcus and airline caterer Sky-Chefs, Inc. brought their people processes into line with their actions.

CHALLENGE: Integrate for Action

Actions can cross multiple boundaries—cultural and national, company, functional, or business unit. And these boundaries may become barriers to action, said 44 percent of those we surveyed. In Chapter 10, we explain—and illustrate with examples from Braun, Bristol-Myers Squibb, and others—how to surmount the boundaries by constructing bridges, while not burning any of them.

CHALLENGE: **Wire for Action**

Information technology is increasingly integral—and increasingly an obstacle—to action. For example, some 35 percent of our survey respondents complained that long technology lead times get in the way of action. In Chapter 11, we give you the tools you need to manage the organization issues technology presents in any action. These tools were tested at Adaptec, Siemens Medical Systems (a subsidiary of Siemens AG), and others.

CHALLENGE: **Reenergize for Action**

Fatigue can kill an action, 32 percent of our survey respondents believe. So, in Chapter 12, we offer insights and examples from copier manufacturer Ricoh Company, Ltd. and others on how to keep your action going.

The Global Action Survey also led us to divide actions into four types: simple actions of short duration, complex actions of short duration, complex actions of long duration, and simple actions of long duration. One of these will have relevance to the project or initiative—the action—that your business is undertaking.

But for now, forget business.

Think Olympic competition: The sprint is a flat-out race from the blocks to the finish. The high jump starts with a short approach run and climaxes with a leap over the bar. The decathlon tests all-around strength and endurance. The marathon demands savvy and stamina over the long haul.

Also consider the athletes in each event: the tightly muscled sprinter, the sinewy jumper, the well-proportioned decathlete, and the lean marathon runner. Each models human form following function, function merging into form. The results are beauty and efficiency, challenges met and mastered, great deeds done.

We said forget business but we bet you didn't, because athletic action so strongly suggests business action. Indeed, business has its own *sprint* (low-complexity actions of short duration), *high jump* (high-complexity actions of short duration), *decathlon* (high-complexity actions of long duration), and *marathon* (low-complexity actions of long duration). Following the paths associated with these four types of action will guide you to peak business performance.

What is your path to action? The goal of this book is your success and the success of your enterprise. To help you gain it, we give you clear, proven methods. The deeds will follow.

The succeeding chapters present action management not just as theory but as practical techniques derived from real companies around the world that faced challenges, sought performance improvements, and achieved them through well-managed action. The victories they won can be yours. Let the games begin.

2

ACTION IS AS ACTION DOES

We classify actions into four types.
These types aren't masks to hide behind,
or costumes to put on. They are departure points
for the journey to peak business performance.

Item: In May 1998 Dow Jones & Company sells Telerate, the financial information services business it acquired earlier in the 1980s, for some $510 million in cash and stock. Unfortunately for Dow Jones, that amount is nowhere near the $1.6 billion it paid for the business. Hefty write-offs associated with the sale produce the first-ever quarterly losses for the venerable publisher of *The Wall Street Journal.*

Item: Alfred J. Dunlap is fired as chairman and chief executive officer of Sunbeam Corporation after his take-no-prisoners, slash-and-burn downsizing fails to return the appliance maker to profitability. Although his elimination of half of Sunbeam's 12,000-person workforce temporarily buoyed the stock price, his methods almost sank the corporate ship in a sea of debt.

Item: Deutsche Bank reins in its free-spending Deutsche Morgan Grenfell investment-banking subsidiary after DMG fails in its efforts to expand its global reach in corporate finance. Bankers depart, offices are closed around the world, and the parent company announces that it will take a $1.5 billion restructuring charge and do away with some 9,000 jobs over a 3-year period.

Browse any business magazine or newspaper, and stories like these, stories of failed acquisitions, failed downsizings, and failed expansions—in a word, failed actions—leap out. The key to successful action, we argue in this chapter, is to follow the right path—and we do mean path.

The four action paths that we identified from our Global Action Survey are based on two key factors: *complexity* and *duration.*

The sprint entails a low-complexity action of short duration. The high jump is a high-complexity action of short duration. The decathlon refers to high-complexity actions of long duration. And, finally, the marathon involves a low-complexity action of long duration.

In the pages that follow, we describe the four action paths in more detail and provide case studies that typify the issues managers face along the way. We'll begin with the sprint.

What Is a Sprint?

Jogging around the business track, you hear footsteps from behind. Suddenly, a rival pulls up alongside, then blows by you. That does it.

No one is going to leave you in their slipstream.

Suddenly, it isn't a Sunday jog anymore. It is a race, a toe-to-toe competition. You are in a sprint, meaning an action that is short in duration (less than two years) and low in complexity.

Outsourcing a single function is a typical sprint. So is functional downsizing or bringing a new product to market.

As an accustomed market leader, you may not be used to this mad dash. But you know what you must do: Kick into high gear.

Nothing complex here. Just straightforward action delivered at a breakneck pace. Of course, motion causes turbulence, and some jobs may be lost. But if you stop to save them, the race will be over and your rival may win the day.

To better understand what a sprint involves, let's take a look at a company that actually made the dash.

▶ ─────────────────────────────────────

LEARN BY EXAMPLE: Adaptec, Inc.

With $1 billion in annual sales, Adaptec, Inc. (www.adaptec.com), of Milpitas, California, is the world's leading producer of hardware and software for speeding the transfer of data between computers, peripherals, and networks.

It makes, among other products, so-called scuzzy devices—the colloquial term derived from the acronym *SCSI*, for small computer system interface. These devices enable personal computers, workstations, and servers to deliver large files and electronic information to peripherals, such as disks, CD recorders, and other data storage systems.

Adaptec's customers include such big-name computer makers as Compaq Computer Corporation, Dell Computer Corporation, and International Business Machines Corporation. In 1995, it racked up its 44th consecutive profitable quarter and posted full-year revenues of $659 million.

This company could breathe easy, right?

Wrong.

Adaptec's explosive growth was blowing apart its own existing business processes and information systems. As Jim Schmidt, vice president of corporate processes and infrastructure development, told us, "Our processes and automation weren't integrated, real-time, scalable, or extendable. That meant we couldn't manage and sustain our own growth. We couldn't reach our goal of surpassing $1 billion in annual sales."

Seizing on internal opportunity, in February 1996 Adaptec executives adopted a program designed by its Singapore operation. Called

Adaptec Process Excellence, or Apex, it became the core for an expanded, companywide overhaul of processes and systems—one that would support its $1-billion-plus sales goal.

The Singapore manufacturing facility had embarked on this continuous-improvement program in 1995 as a way to incrementally reduce costs by cutting product development and production time. Although Singapore's objectives, and even its Apex program name, were to be retained, its continuous-improvement approach was not.

Adaptec's culture embraces speed. It is a born sprinter—and "a very aggressive company," in the words of Gina Gloski, director of manufacturing. "We can't tolerate a project longer than 18 months," she says. "It is just not the culture."

Accordingly, a three-member executive review board was appointed to make rapid decisions. The prime concern was scheduling.

Clearly, the need for short program duration ruled out decathlon or marathon actions. Moreover, the complexities of diverse processes and international and functional boundaries seemed to rule out a simple sprint.

But did they really?

Adaptec worked to lessen complexity by building bridges across functions. Schmidt, with strong support from business, service, and technical areas—and backed 100 percent by senior management—was appointed Apex project manager. His objectives were clearly defined: A 12-month schedule was the priority.

Project control was centralized at U.S. headquarters, but process-owner representatives from Singapore were included. Most employees at the Asian facility spoke English, so language wasn't a barrier. Still, cultural differences between East and West were significant.

"American business culture is different," observes Esther Chia, Singapore team leader. "People are more direct and speak their minds. In Asia, we have opinions, but we are more quiet. We hold onto our concerns. At first, Americans think we take a lot of time to begin action, but we are just still thinking."

Chia says she helped people be more frank and vocal in early meetings. "It is an adjustment, but it's good for people to grow and understand different cultures," she says, "so they can work together for a common goal."

Adaptec could have pursued brutal efficiency by forgoing employee involvement. Instead, the company saw people as a valuable resource for getting the job done. Managers viewed their challenge as a sprint that demanded all the committed muscle, heart, and soul they could muster.

In the chapters that follow, we look at how Adaptec ran its rapid race.

◀

What Is a High Jump?

You have taken a hit. Sales have dropped, and market share is declining. Your stock has plunged. Perhaps costs have risen to intolerable levels.

It isn't doomsday yet, but you realize that business performance *must* improve. Rapid action is required. That action may be a merger or acquisition, a radical restructuring, or some other project aimed at corporate revitalization.

Whatever it is, the action is no doubt complex. Yet, it must be of short duration and decisive, because the window of opportunity is open just a crack. It is now or never. You are entered in the high-jump event, and jump you must.

With a high jump—a complex action that takes less than two years from beginning to end—the bar is set on the top rung. It is a long way up. You need powerful muscles for your launch and single-minded focus as you leap.

You must narrow your task by prioritizing your activities. Forget, "What *can* we do to achieve peak business performance?" Think, "What *must* we do to achieve peak business performance?"

This is Olympic drama, and you can smell victory ahead.

Some people, though, fear for their jobs. Don't ignore them. Rally them around the common purpose. Remind them that it is everyone's gain if you succeed, everyone's loss if you fail. Let them know where you—and they—stand.

And make it clear, as did the executives and managers at Bank Corporation, a client in the financial services industry that wishes to remain anonymous, that success demands unified, full-time commitment.

▶ ───

LEARN BY EXAMPLE: **Bank Corporation***

When 1996 benchmarking data on business performance placed the finance arm of Bank Corporation in the bottom 25 percent of its industry, President Daniel Wright knew big moves were required.

Why shouldn't Bank Corporation be in the top 25 percent? Why not, indeed?

To that end, Wright ordered his finance department to slash costs by some 40 percent within a year—by May 1998.

Coincidentally, remembers Kaitlin Fisher, manager of the action, the finance department was already at work on a plan to reduce its expenses—but by only 20 percent. Wright dismissed that goal as inadequate.

The tricky part, Wright and Fisher knew, was to slash costs while maintaining quality. The bank could not afford to do otherwise. If quality suffered, the entire organization would be jeopardized.

---

* This firm wished to remain anonymous, so its name and the names of its officers have been changed.

The challenge for finance, then, was to leap into action, and quickly. In other words, it had to execute a high jump.

Reactions were mixed.

For one thing, Bank Corporation was profitable. So there was no perceived burning need, despite the grim benchmarking data, for massive upheaval.

Besides, finance had tried to take action before—four times before, to be exact. Each attempt to clear the high bar had failed. The kind of radical action demanded by Wright always seemed to elude the finance operation.

To combat initial resistance and get people on board quickly, Fisher sponsored a series of workshops for groups of 25 to 50 employees. They were asked to come up with ways the action might be structured. As ideas flowed, people began to believe that finance could, for the first time, carry off a high jump.

The action called for centralizing all of finance, more than 2,000 full-time employees, in 40 work groups, under the leadership of controller Jonathon Gross. To implement the new structure, almost all U.S.-based finance employees—some 1,200 people—had to be reassigned.

Not surprisingly, the redeployment provoked enormous anxiety. But Wright and Fisher assured people that they would have an equal shot at holding current jobs or obtaining new ones. In the end, the process was fair—and fast.

The huge reshuffling of employees was accomplished in only three months. The speedy resolution kept disruption to a minimum while averting the anger and productivity losses that can take root when people are left in limbo.

Three things characterized the Bank Corporation action: (1) an explicit goal of business performance, (2) a definite and aggressive timetable, and (3) participation of line managers coupled with clear accountability. All were key to the action's success.

But to Julia Kuhl, senior vice president of finance, Wright's initial objective was the crucial element. Performance in the top 25 percent via a 40 percent cost reduction "was a goal against industry benchmarks, and it was very, very aggressive," she says. "Putting the two together forced people to work together 'outside the box.'

"The only way you could achieve a goal that aggressive was by leveraging expertise across the organization. So it forced teamwork," Kuhl goes on, "which is why I'm now a huge fan of very aggressive and potentially unrealistic goals. They make people approach challenges differently."

In the chapters that follow, we see how Bank Corporation met its successive challenges and cleared that high-jump bar.

◀

What Is a Decathlon?

Wouldn't it be nice if you were confronted with business challenges one at a time? But you aren't, so you find yourself pursuing a series of mettle-testing events.

In business, as in track and field, the decathlon is the most grueling event of all—highly complex and of long duration. How can you win a decathlon? Are you superhuman? Well, if the cross-training shoe fits. . . .

Action like this may be new. You have never faced so many challenges at once.

Perhaps you are reaching for long-term market leadership by taking innovative action. Maybe there are multiple pieces, including a strong cultural or behavioral component. There is an international dimension, too. And everything has to be phased in over three or four stages.

Corporate transformations involving new structures, processes, products, markets, and systems—basically complete overhauls—are definitely decathlon events. So, too, are the privatization of government organizations and the establishment of international shared-service centers.

To win a decathlon, your vision must correspond with your abilities. You have to build on your strengths and expand your range.

▶————————————————————————————

LEARN BY EXAMPLE: **British Airways Engineering**

British Airways Engineering is the world's largest and most experienced aircraft-engineering business. Besides maintaining 250 planes for British Airways, it also looks after the aircraft of more than 100 other operators worldwide.

The impetus for action came in 1995 when British Airways decided that BA Engineering should become an independent supplier, operating on a commercial contract basis. Forced to make a move, the company opted for a big one. It set out to dramatically redesign its business to achieve world-class levels of performance.

The transformation demanded significant action at every level of BA Engineering's 9,500-member workforce. Business processes, work patterns, structures, systems, culture—you name it, it had to be altered.

For simplicity's sake, the massive maneuver was labeled "Reengineering Our Future." But the highly complex action, which would require a minimum of three years to complete, was anything but simple.

"Finding any one person who was able to grasp the whole of it was very difficult because it was so large," observes Keith Mitchell, fleet general manager. "The main problem in our minds was, how do we maintain the operation at a particular level of airworthiness in the midst of the changeover?"

A strong transition team of 80 full-time employees was established to satisfy two goals: first, to maximize involvement in the redesign process; and, second, to harvest best practices worldwide.

Indicative of the team's success, some 1,500 people actively participated in the action's design. And design teams visited more than 40 companies to discover best practices.

One of the project team's first tasks was to analyze the organization's readiness and ability to transform itself. The team was then able to pinpoint areas that threatened to delay or derail the initiative. Key issues revolved around eradicating functional boundaries and reengineering an old-style, task-oriented operation.

Substantial stakeholder-involvement and communications activities were carried out during this early phase, too. Following a launch briefing, initial interviews were undertaken with over 200 key stakeholders to discuss views on direction, possible issues, and how people wished to participate further. Extensive brainstorming workshops were run to contribute new ideas.

All of these initiatives served to increase support of and commitment to the reengineering effort, which was critical to its success.

Although the program is on track to completion within its three-year time span, success has not come without some disruption and pain. Looking back, Brian Philpott, who was acting managing director when the action began and is now technical director and responsible for maintaining the integrity of the fleets, says that the entire program was "much larger than we thought."

BA Engineering is an extremely complex, interdependent business with equally complex processes. "I think we underestimated the complexity," Philpott says.

Time has also been a factor: "We had to improve our performance and get into the markets before they evaporated or were occupied by somebody else." But Philpott believes that speed is essential, no matter what. "If you allow things to get too strung out, you lose sight of the objective and will probably never reach it," he says.

In the pages ahead, we examine how BA Engineering maintained its focus and pushed on to the finish line during the grueling, all-around competition that is a decathlon.

◀

What Is a Marathon?

Ever run a 100-yard dash? Or the quarter-mile? You are pushing flat-out all the way, legs churning, muscles burning. Who could run a whole mile, you wonder. Five miles? Twenty-six?

You could, and sometimes you have to when you determine that your action strategy needs to drill a long-term orientation deep into the heart of the business.

Don't despair. There is a method to the marathon madness. The method is one step at a time as you persevere through many stages and all kinds of weather.

Departing from a detailed blueprint, you roll out actions area by area. You limit customization while still holding to a common overall agenda and set of action principles. This approach lets you effect cultural shifts and develop new competencies in measured stages.

For example, you can inject a customer focus into your front-office organization, introduce shareholder value management, and reengineer entire processes and departments without overloading the organization. The key is pacing and establishing a rhythm by linking many small, simple actions to longer-term goals, which often lie 5, even 10 years ahead.

Over time, you need to make sure that these actions touch a wide enough area so that people, processes, the organization as a whole, technology, customers, and facilities are all advancing toward a shared vision of the business.

Long-term effort takes its toll, of course—in employee energy, focus, and commitment. Your corunners will be few, because your business can't spare large numbers for special long-term action projects. Indeed, your line managers will shoulder most of the load.

You must keep everyone in the race. Guide and support them, but take care not to micromanage their day-to-day implementation of the action.

Here's how one company does it.

▶ _____

LEARN BY EXAMPLE: Kawasaki Heavy Industries, Ltd.

At Kawasaki Heavy Industries, Ltd. (www.khi.co.jp/index.html) in Kobe, Japan, change never stops—and, therefore, neither does action. The driver of action is the imperative to reduce material and labor costs. It remains constant, as does Kawasaki's view that one improvement is merely a step toward another.

Although action is constant and connected, it isn't aimed at all problems at once. Each challenge is treated as unique. Kawasaki targets areas where costs can be reduced or quality upgraded. Action is designed to improve performance, and then is implemented incrementally over two to five years.

Clearly, this $8.4-billion-a-year engineering conglomerate doesn't enter high-jump or sprint competitions. But does it run the decathlon? The marathon?

The clues are in the action's complexity.

At first glance, an ever-changing workplace might seem tipped toward instability, even chaos. Kawasaki's small central action team keeps firm control, though, by coordinating training and transferring learning to the whole organization.

Each operational unit also has its own business-improvement team. The Akashi motorcycle group business-improvement team, for example, has 20 members. The Banshu Construction Machinery business-improvement team has 15. In addition, the company president visits all factories twice a year to get a detailed view and set precise targets.

Senior managers, who are responsible for delivery of benefits, are motivated by targets that grow more demanding each year. Failure to deliver is seen not as a failure of the front line, but as a failure of leaders. They bear full responsibility because they are in full control.

Employee compliance is expected and received. As Takashi Fujiura, director and deputy senior general manager of the rolling stock group, explains, "Action is a top-down movement. Top management decides what is required."

Lest this seem like bald dictatorship, note that employees have plenty of incentive to follow directives.

First, their employment is secure. If tasks are eliminated by new efficiencies, affected employees are reassigned, never fired. By the same token, highly efficient operations mean that less work is outsourced, and that creates jobs. Long service is rewarded with promotions. Wages steadily rise as the company's fixed costs drop with inventory and storage-space reductions.

Because individual departments are assigned discrete targets, functional boundaries aren't an issue, which further lessens action complexity. Overseas entities, such as the motorcycle distributorships and ship-repair factories, are expected to follow the same action procedures as the Japanese units, thus ensuring international coordination.

Suppliers' quality and costs are kept in line by aggressive value analysis and price negotiation. When products or prices prove unsatisfactory, new suppliers are found or the work is brought in-house.

Our overview shows that Kawasaki is a distance runner whose thoroughgoing management of complexity, connections, and detail makes its races marathons.

Striding forward one step at a time, limiting its focus to each single task at hand, and streamlining its efforts to contain costs and resources, Kawasaki is a corporate giant that runs long by running lean.

Norio Harada, associate director of the construction machinery division, explains the company's success in human terms: "The biggest reason for improvement is as much the strong will of senior management as the action techniques themselves."

Later, as we race along with Kawasaki, we will see further evidence of how will and technique have carried this company on its way.

◀

What Is Your Path to Action?

Now let's zero in on the type of action—sprint, high jump, decathlon, or marathon—that is right for you.

A runner can't consciously analyze every factor of the course as the starter raises the gun. But on the business track, you can.

First, consider the factors that influence the *complexity* of your action. Then, consider the factors that influence the *duration* of your action.

How Complex Is Your Action?

We know from experience that you can't manage an action or identify your action path without understanding its complexity. So we put together a test that allows you to gauge that.

First, though, a few basics.

Several factors determine an action's complexity. Among them is the number of people involved. Less is less, at least when it comes to complexity.

Our rule of thumb: *The more people affected, the more complex the action.* And be sure to include both customers and employees in your tally.

Ask yourself: How many customers will be substantially affected by my action? How will they be affected? Likewise, how many employees will be substantially affected—meaning retrained for new duties or at least reoriented to a changed role? Will it be 100? 1,000? 10,000 or more?

Will your action dramatically shift decision-making control? Actions that empower employees or decentralize authority will do just that, and these shifts boost the level of complexity.

Aspirations also influence an action's complexity. Again, less is less. If you aim to catapult your organization to a much higher level of business performance, be prepared for greater complication.

Our rule of thumb: *The greater the performance improvement you seek, the more complex the action.*

Still another factor that determines complexity is scope. Common sense tells us—and our Global Action Survey backs us up—that the more variables you add into the mix, the more complex an action program becomes.

Consider the number of processes affected by an action, and the accompanying technological ramifications. Ask yourself, too, how many functions, countries, and business units will be involved. Need we tell you that the more widespread the involvement, the greater the complexity?

Discovering that your action is highly complex need not bring you grief, however. The only time complexity is life threatening to your action is when it catches you unaware. Action is always easier if you know what to expect.

We have designed the quiz in Figure 2.1 to alert you to potential problems. Put pencil to paper, and discover how complex your action is.

How Long Will Your Action Last?

The basic notion of duration, or the amount of time an action takes, is easy to understand. We all grapple with having too little time to accomplish our goals, or we sense that time passes too quickly.

How Complex Is Your Planned Action?

Use this quiz to make a quick assessment of your action program's complexity. The higher the score, the more complex the action. Knowing the level of complexity is the first step toward determining which action path is right for you.

Ask yourself	1 Point	2 Points	3 Points
How many of the organization's employees will be substantially affected by my action?*	Fewer than 1,000	1,000 to 10,000	More than 10,000
How will customers be affected by my action?	Little if any impact	Service level and way of doing business will change.	Product, way of doing business, and service level will change.
How large is the anticipated performance improvement from my action?	Moderate	Substantial	Leap to world class
How large is the anticipated power shift?†	Modest	Moderate	Dramatic
How many different business processes will be significantly changed in my action?‡	1	2 or 3	4 or more

(continued)

Substantially means that a person's job content changes enough to require additional training, reorientation, and face-to-face communication.

†Power resides in decision-making authority, control of resources, and influence on the business. Senior leadership changes, centralization or decentralization, empowerment, procedures that tighten controls, and restructuring, among other things, all produce power shifts.

‡Business processes are as defined in a value chain (that is, in-bound logistics, manufacturing, procurement, and so forth). *Significantly changed* implies considerable process change on top of any changes needed to accommodate new systems.

Figure 2.1   Action complexity assessment.

Ask yourself	1 Point	2 Points	3 Points
What kind of changes to technology will be made as part of my action?*	Minor new applications	Major new applications	New architecture
How many different functions will my action affect?†	1	2 to 5	More than 5
How many major countries will my action affect?	1	2 to 5	More than 5
How many different locations are impacted by my action?‡	Fewer than 5	5 to 10	More than 10
How will the business culture need to be changed to support my action?¶	Little change (Are you sure? Check again.)	Moderate change in behavior	Transformation in behavior
Total Complexity score = _____			

*Minor new applications would include the addition of specialist software, such as a financial evaluation package, for example. Enterprisewide resource-planning (ERP) systems are an example of a major application.

†Functions, as used here, include finance, human resources, information technology, sales, marketing, customer service, and distribution.

‡Locations means substantial centers only. Don't count retail outlets or small distribution facilities.

¶The business culture is defined by employee values, behaviors, and general mind-set.

Figure 2.1   Continued.

But determining the duration of an action is made more difficult when the question becomes not "How long will it take?" but "How long have you got?"

The chief executive officer of one of our client companies in Europe articulated the dilemma every leader faces. "I don't like having to move this fast," he told his senior management team, "demanding that you deal with strategy, today's performance, and changing the culture all at the same time. I don't like it any more than you do.

"But we have no choice," he added. "Our shareholders won't wait for us to introduce the changes at a pace that feels comfortable to us."

What this chief executive knows—and what you must know, too—is that the duration of your action will most likely be determined by two competing forces: pressure from customers and shareholders to improve performance, and the ability of the organization to deliver.

The questions are thorny ones. How long will your shareholders wait for you to boost the stock price or increase dividends? How long will your customers stick around while you work to upgrade a product? How quickly can employees learn the new technology that is the backbone of your action?

Also, how compelling is your case for action? How is it perceived, not only by shareholders and customers, but also by your workforce? If you can convince all of them that your action is valuable, they, in turn, are more likely to give you the benefit of the doubt—and the benefit of time.

Looking backward has value, too. Knowing how long it took your company to complete previous actions is a good indicator of what to expect this time around. After all, organizations have their own internal clocks. Trying to pull off a sprint at a company that is a natural long-distance runner is bound to cause delays and disappointments, if not failure.

Another point to consider: According to our global survey, *duration is linked to both the degree of technological change and the degree of culture change involved.* In a business action—any business action—the greater the changes, the more time required.

What's more, questions must be asked about resource availability. It doesn't matter whether resources are actually scarce or whether someone has failed to make a timely assessment of their availability. In either case, your action will be delayed.

Answering these questions goes a long way toward clarifying how ready your business is to implement an action.

In any event, expect the final word on duration to vary from early esti-mates. Virtually every company we have observed expects to accomplish its actions in 12 to 18 months. But as planning progresses, a company realizes how much time the action will actually take. Two or two and a half years starts to sound reasonable—then three to four years is floated.

Eventually, the need to keep the project at a more manageable level leads to a reverse of the process. Competing demands of customers, shareholders, and employees force the team to scale back the action and tighten time estimates.

To help you approximate the duration of your action, we put together the test in Figure 2.2.

What Is Your Path to Action? (Redux)

You are ready to choose your action path.

Your scores on the complexity and duration quizzes allow you to plot your position on the action-path grid shown in Figure 2.3. The position determines your action path: sprint, high jump, decathlon, or marathon.

Now the perils and opportunities are clarified and the strategies for managing them to your best business advantage are defined. You are ready to train your view on the finish-line tape as the starter raises the gun.

Questions and Answers

QUESTION: What if my quiz results place my action in the middle of the path diagram?

There is no overall right or wrong position on the grid, only what is right for the business challenge you are facing. However, if your answers put you in a position located close to the center of the grid, you must make a judgment. Ask yourself: What is the most discrimi-

How Long Will Your Action Take?

Use this quiz to make a quick assessment of your action program's duration. The higher the score, the longer the action will take. Knowing the timetable is the second step toward determining which action path is right for you.

Ask yourself	1 Point	2 Points	3 Points
How compelling is the perceived reason for my action?	Highly compelling (by crisis or inspiration)	People see and agree on the case	Logical but little urgency created by the case
How long will the marketplace give me to deliver improvements? (Based on your knowledge of investor, competitor, and customer activity, as well as market trends.)	Less than one year (Are you sure? Look again at complexity.)	One to two years	More than two years
How long did the last major action program take to deliver improvements in my company?	Less than two years	More than two years	No comparable experience
How central to my action are changes in technology or culture?	Modest components only	Important enablers of the change	Represent the key changes
Where do I stand on action program resources? (Key resources include people, finances, and facilities.)	Resources obtained	Resources promised, not yet obtained	Lots of ideas, no resources
How ready is my organization for the action?	People want this action now	Half ready; half not	Come back next year!
Total Duration score = _____			

Figure 2.2   Action duration assessment.

nating feature of my action path, complexity or duration? Whichever side you come down on will dictate your position in one of the quadrants, thus indicating the type of action path you should follow.

Finding yourself in the center of the grid is in no way problematic. Rather, it simply reflects the fact that many elements of different action programs are similar, and you can learn something from all of them. But while learning from the similarities, it's important to realize that the

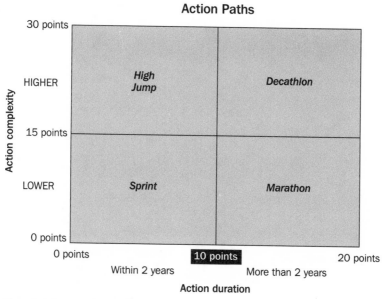

Figure 2.3   Action-path grid.

main reason for categorizing your action path is to uncover the differences, because the differences will determine whether or not you are adequately tailoring events to meet the specific needs of your organization.

QUESTION: Is it enough to know an action's path?

No. There are a number of prerequisites for successful action. In the early stages of any action, we believe you must have three things:

1. A clear vision of what you want to achieve.

2. Commitment and support from your leaders.

3. A credible business case that proves the strategic and operational benefits of your action. The business case also needs to estimate the likely cost of the action.

Once these prerequisites are in place, you are ready to begin planning your action—the subject of the next chapter.

MANAGEMENT IS ACTION

The 10 challenges every action manager faces.

CHAPTER

3

THE FIRST CHALLENGE—
PLAN FOR ACTION

Down to business. Time to start. What comes first?
An action plan. Why an action plan? Read on.

It was to be the largest suspension bridge in the world, crossing New York's East River in one unbroken span and measuring a mile from the beginning of one onshore approach to the end of the other. Everything about the structure that engineer John Augustus Roebling proposed was wondrous.

And every detail was contained in his plan.

Just as Roebling didn't build the Brooklyn Bridge without a blueprint, a director doesn't shoot a movie without a script, and a pilot doesn't take off without a clearly marked route, neither can you undertake an action without a plan. What is your blueprint? Your script? Your plan?

We won't leave you up in the air flying by the seat of your pants on just theory, a wing, and a prayer. We will lead you through a step-by-step methodology drawn from first-hand experience and exhaustive research into planning for business actions.

What you create is more than just a document. It is a catalyst for change. And change is movement. Movement is action. Action is advantage.

To assure that you achieve the advantage you want, we show you in this chapter how to define an action's necessity and objective, choose your strategy, establish participants' roles, set realistic time schedules, and build organizational support.

And because we know that good managers look at the upside, the downside, and the upside down, we also show you how to keep the plan on track through all the stages of an action—from implementation to completion. We address the risks, the benefits, the costs, and the availability and allocation of resources associated with adopting specific strategies.

To be sure, the road of action winds crazily sometimes. Hazards loom ahead that may delay you, but they will never force you off the road. You have marked the route, and you have a compass.

Uphill and down the journey goes. But, as the Chinese say, even a thousand-mile trek starts with a single step. That first step is the plan.

A well-designed action plan is a concise, compelling document. It lays out the *why,* the *what,* the *how,* and the *who* of an action.

That is, it presents the business need and lists clear, measurable objectives. It sets up an implementation schedule and marks the milestones along the way. It also establishes the duties, accountabilities, and time requirements of action team members. And it addresses resource allocation issues. Above all, the action plan embodies the approval of senior managers, whose commitment is essential.

Action Tips

Here are our tips for making and managing your action plan.

TIP▶ Choose Your Strategy

The work of developing your strategy takes place during the initiation stage of your action. Strategy is driven by business need, and it involves, in the broadest sense, choosing between two options: *all at once,* or *one step at a time.*

Sprints and high jumps lend themselves to all-at-once strategies; decathlons and marathons to one-step-at-a-time strategies. Whichever you choose—and neither is universally correct—assumptions about risks, resources, and time frames need to be spelled out in your plan.

Why do you—like Adaptec, Inc.—want to do it all at once? Let us count the reasons.

1. The business need is so severe that you must.

2. The action is so complex that you are forced to group activities together.

3. There is consistency among the various activities—across geography, organization, and culture.

What's good about doing it all at once?

Our experience is that, once made, these actions stick. And they can alleviate common communication problems, such as the difficulty of sustaining interest and momentum over long periods of preparation or off-line work, when nothing much appears to be happening.

On the downside, all-at-once strategies are often resource intensive. They also may tax an organization's management and technical expertise up to and even beyond its capabilities.

Why do you want to do it one step at a time?

1. Errors and mistakes are identified earlier, with less severe consequences.

2. Business continuity isn't prejudiced because pilot implementations are a far less risky, "toe-in-the-water" approach.

3. The extent of any backtracking is relatively minor, with minimal waste of time or resources.

4. Learning is maximized, because each successive rollout is usually smoother than the one that preceded it.

You might be surprised to learn that one-step-at-a-time strategies aren't necessarily for the faint of heart. They have a broader applicability within action management than is usually appreciated—especially when, as our survey found, 35 percent of all action programs take more than 2 years to deliver any benefits.

Some of the most successful actions we encountered were by companies that set about to accomplish their plans incrementally—as we will see later in the example of Braun, the Gillette Company subsidiary.

▶ _____

LEARN BY EXAMPLE: Adaptec, Inc.

It's no surprise that management at computer peripheral manufacturer Adaptec adopted an all-at-once strategy. In the computer industry, such a strategy is the norm.

And Adaptec—with a product life cycle of only 12 to 18 months and revenue growth topping 40 percent annually—is a classic sprinter.

We asked Paul Hansen, chief financial officer, to explain how the company went about planning its reengineering and its system action program. Here's what he told us:

> We went around and researched other major business process reengineering undertakings. We noted that the ones that tried to get it done in less than 12 months limited the scope so tremendously that they really crippled their ability to make quantum breakthrough progress. The ones that let it drag on beyond two years started losing focus—team members wanted to rotate off the project, as they didn't want to spend more than two years of their

careers on something like this. So, scientifically, we figured that some point in between one year and two years was about the appropriate time.

LEARN BY EXAMPLE: Braun

When Braun, the German consumer electronics subsidiary of Gillette, simultaneously reengineered its business processes and incorporated them within an enterprisewide SAP system, a one-step-at-a-time strategy was fundamental to its success.

In fact, Dieter Timmerman, project manager, told us that an all-at-once implementation was never an option. "Resource constraints wouldn't allow it, the consequences of failure would have been disastrous, and important learning experiences would have been missed," Timmerman says.

"A successful pilot allowed us to establish credibility with a quick win, while learning what we could in a manageable environment."

That said, Timmerman notes that the particular choice of where to implement the pilot is critical. "We decided to implement first in our Scandinavian subsidiary," he relates.

"It was a big enough market that we could test both the new processes and the software in a meaningful way. But not too big, so the degree of risk was one that we could live with.

"What's more, Scandinavia comprises several countries, so the implementation actually mirrored the overall Braun implementation—with different languages, different cultures, different currencies, and different processes."

Even so, Timmerman was careful to first establish that the Scandinavian operation was up to the task. "We weren't wanting to test the local management's ability to absorb stress—just the SAP software and our own redesigned processes," he says.

"Both management and employees were in good shape: settled, stable, and competent. And the culture was open, too. There were going to be learning points, and we wanted to make sure that we captured as many of them as possible," Timmerman adds.

Piloting actions in a test bed, as Braun did, helps minimize risk, as does phasing in actions over time so as to balance resource requirements, risk, and the speed of delivery of the anticipated benefits.

That way, dramatic—even, in some cases, revolutionary—improvements are delivered in an evolutionary way. Fewer resources are used, but the time frames can be similar to those achieved in organizations where the all-at-once approach is applied.

TIP▶ Develop and Own an Action Vision

The key to action planning is the clear articulation by senior managers of what they expect the business to look like three years out. That means creating a vision, then breaking it down into tasks that can be accomplished.

In the analysis stage, you, as action manager, learn where your company is and what needs to be improved. During definition, you specify what your action program will do to bring about that improvement.

Some advice: Remember that this is senior management's vision, not yours.

As action manager, you are the master of implementation. You probably don't own the resources or have the authority to tell the organization what to do. You facilitate the action, leveraging the case for action as stated by your chief executive and his or her team.

On the other hand, you most likely are the one who determines what the vision really means. In our experience, the action manager inherits the task of clarifying the vision before definition can begin.

Again, though, don't misplay your hand. It's critical that you gain senior management's backing for your interpretation. Everyone must be headed in the same direction.

TIP▶ Divide Your Action into Manageable Parts for Planning

The fuzzy edges of your action plan should disappear in the definition stage. The detail accumulated along the way brings your action into sharp focus.

The accuracy of the plan depends on how well you define it. How do you get started, though, when you know the details won't be filled in until later?

First, think of the four key parts of your action plan as a series of documents:

1. A clear statement of the business need

2. A master schedule of activities

3. The organization structure of the project

4. A statement of the resources required to deliver the action

Then, describe the four parts as a series of logical projects.

As action manager, your role here is a guiding one. The responsibility for delivering each piece falls to individual managers. They are your lieutenants in the campaign to achieve the vision. They define what is required at the activity, task, and subtask levels.

By *activities,* we mean the primary initiatives of an action. *Tasks* are what must be done in between clear starting and ending dates. A *subtask* is detailed work, probably of short duration, but work that you feel needs to be tracked.

How to proceed? Start by taking your action and breaking it into discrete projects. Then, identify the dependencies among the projects and focus on managing the linkages.

The overall program plan takes precedence here in determining the action's critical path—that is, how long the action will take to complete after you estimate the duration of each project.

In turn, your program managers break their projects into work packages that allow for clear measurement of interim deliverables.

By using this breakdown structure, you bring the action right down to the task level. There are distinct benefits.

For one, you involve project managers in delineating their areas of responsibility. Also, there is a disciplined approach to identifying and linking the tasks that are required to achieve the program deliverables.

Further, it becomes clear that your role is to resolve conflict and resource issues at the boundaries. And, finally, control, planning, and reporting are integrated across the organization.

TIP▶ Make a Plan on a Page

When you have defined your action, you then want to create a plan for transition. Your accumulated knowledge may lead you to decide that the transition should be broken into stages that go on for several years.

Ideally, the planning process at this point provides you with a *plan on a page*. That's a one-page overview of what you expect to achieve, with periodic milestones spelled out—say, for every quarter. Supplementing that broad outline will be a more detailed view of the first six months set down in a Gantt chart format.

▶───────────────────────────────

LEARN BY EXAMPLE: British Airways Engineering

From the beginning, it was apparent that BA Engineering's reengineering would be a huge undertaking, what with some 9,500 people being affected and the whole organization being reengineered.

What wasn't apparent was exactly how complex the planning would become.

"The project team started at 45 people for planning and grew to 300 people at its peak," recalls project manager Ray Claydon. And if 45 sounds like a lot of people to draw up a plan—and Claydon admits that some companies he's spoken to "are frightened by this level of commitment"—he quickly ticks off a convincing array of reasons.

"This was a massive action and one single person just cannot grasp all the complexities involved. And don't forget, we had a business that had to continue to operate—and one with highly specific needs. The plan not only needed to ensure the continuity of the operation, but there were also legally stipulated airworthiness requirements to observe."

Risk avoidance was therefore of paramount importance. But the level of complexity is not always controllable.

In this case, rough outline plans had uncovered a high level of interdependency among many of the required actions, a fact that made a one-step-at-a-time approach particularly difficult.

Claydon points out that a critical learning point in planning massive actions is the need to allow more time for the planning process itself. "I mean, if 9,500 people are to all have a new job, just think of the number of interviews that have to be carried out and job-related process descriptions prepared and training carried out.

"Not everyone is going to have exactly the right mix of skills for their new role," Claydon points out.

Not that progress at BA Engineering hasn't been excellent.

Some three years into the implementation plan, "we're only a few weeks off target," enthuses Keith Mitchell, fleet general manager. Perhaps predictably, the shortfall has largely been in training, which, in turn, contributes to a slower-than-anticipated acceleration in maintenance productivity.

◄

TIP▶ Keep Your Plan Flexible

Planning is an ongoing activity. You continuously improve the tasks to be completed as the body of available knowledge increases.

You reach the end of one action stage and you revise the plan for the next stage based on the knowledge you gain. You cycle through your plan in time increments that represent logical achievements.

A good plan is derived from quality information and knowledge-based assumptions. If assumptions change as knowledge grows, then the plan changes, too.

The constant state of flux may seem like an excuse to let delivery dates slip. It isn't.

You must meet your milestones. Sloppy handling of incremental goals sends a dangerous message to stakeholders and threatens the overall success of the action.

TIP▶ Use a Traffic-Light Approach to Manage Your Plan

As we said before, the planning process is iterative. The plan is continually fine-tuned as issues arise and solutions are presented. We use what we call a *traffic-light approach*.

A *red* light is automatically triggered when there is any concern that deliverables will not be met and no backup plan is in place. Stop everything until a way to remedy the situation is devised.

The light flashes *yellow* in marginal situations when there is some lack of confidence in the action plan. Proceed cautiously and keep a close watch on problem resolution, making sure that expected results are arriving on schedule.

The light turns *green* when you are confident that the plan will meet all milestones and deliverables. All systems are go.

The skill in managing action lies in the ability to track and manage progress. If the requisite capabilities are lacking, you have to develop or hire them.

Action Paths

Here's our advice on planning for your action path.

▶ACTION PATH   Sprint

Set aggressive weekly and monthly milestones, targeting quick wins to gain early credibility.

Accept some uncertainty in planning, so you can move right into action, learning as you go.

Keep the scope of your action—and your action plan—clear and manageable.

Plan for parallel actions where possible.

Sweep your critical path clear and represent it in your plan.

▶ACTION PATH   High Jump

Prioritize efforts based on speed of delivery and projected market impact, eliminating or deferring less important efforts.

Use the plan to merge key actions into a critical mass and stage an ambitious launch.

Plan for a single, early success within 30 days.

Use the plan to signal urgency and rally commitment.

Identify which actions might be stopped or delayed.

▶ACTION PATH   Decathlon

Define and focus on the area of desired performance, and incorporate those insights into your plan.

Simplify your plan and streamline implementation by breaking the larger action into a series of smaller ones.

Set frequent milestones in a three- to five-year plan, linking sequential actions.

Plan international actions and country-by-country rollouts carefully, expecting to encounter complications that will slow down progress.

Use your plan to pilot innovative actions at headquarters to demonstrate that the action is under way and there is no turning back.

▶**ACTION PATH**   **Marathon**

Use your plan to check progress every six to nine months.

Mine the experience of other action managers and their teams, and incorporate their insights into your plan.

Use your plan to sustain momentum—refer to it often, and publicly.

Questions and Answers

QUESTION: Should I plan for quick wins?

Absolutely. Our rule of thumb, which we call the *half-life rule,* is that for every six months that you fail to produce a quick win, the support for your action is reduced by half and employee resistance doubles.

The underlying principle is simple: Actions speak louder than words. Or should we say, *success* speaks louder than words.

Understand, though, that a quick win doesn't mean that the whole action program has to be in place in six months. It simply means that some measurable action must come quickly to keep the troops interested and involved.

At BA Engineering, where the decision to reach for world-class status meant doing away with functional boundaries and operational silos, early reorganization at the top let people know that the action was real. Symbolic but meaningful first steps in the reorganization included doing away with traditional badges of rank and hierarchy, like reserved parking spots and titles on office doors.

Another example: When Adaptec decided to take its Singapore Apex program companywide in 1996, it encountered indifference laced with a belief that the initiative would fall flat.

The objective was to redesign and automate the company's processes. But with two failed attempts to change systems coloring their perception, Adaptec's rank and file people were none too enthusiastic about the latest endeavor.

A few months down the road, though, the project was still alive and people began to take notice.

And then, early in 1997, it became clear not only that the action was serious, but that its implications were big. Suddenly, people wanted information and they wanted to be involved.

One final note of caution: Even though quick wins strengthen the commitment of stakeholders, don't be fooled into thinking that early results are end results. Long-term commitment is ultimately the name of the game.

If you think that you need to plan for only six months, you will fail. Plan for at least two years out, but always with the idea that you will periodically reassess and refresh the plan as events warrant.

QUESTION: What's the biggest issue you face in planning?

How many resources you will be allowed and whether they will be adequate to meet the action program goals on time.

To address this issue, we suggest you use *forward and backward scheduling*. Plan going forward first, determining what it would take to meet your goals. When you find that your end dates are way beyond the time frame, reverse the process and schedule backward while looking at the resource requirements.

You will end up with a profile of the total required resources, total timing, and the key milestones that your project managers believe they can hit.

QUESTION: Is it really possible to come up with a realistic time schedule?

It's tough. One of the most frequent complaints expressed by the 500 managers we surveyed was that action timetables are almost always unrealistic.

Our rule of thumb: *Expect to expand your first estimates of timetables by 50 percent.*

How do you overcome this problem? You need to fully explore how various factors influence the speed of action.

Four of these—(1) the business's action track record, (2) its degree of action saturation, (3) the senior managers' action leadership abilities, and (4) the resources available to implement the action—are specific to the individual case.

Each factor brings its own peculiarities to bear on the process of taking, and planning for, action. In general, though, you want to know how successfully and how quickly previous actions were undertaken.

Also, how many competing actions either are in progress or have recently been completed? How ready and able is senior management to champion these actions? And at what level are necessary skills and resources available?

4

THE SECOND CHALLENGE— ALLOCATE FOR ACTION

How do you secure the resources your program needs to move forward? This chapter provides the answer.

As an action manager, you must take it as an axiom of business life that there are never enough resources—never have been, never will be.

Of the 500 multinational companies we included in our Global Action Survey, some 240 (48 percent) said that competition for scarce resources was a major barrier to action programs. In fact, the action managers we spoke to named the need to compete for resources, particularly people, as the biggest issue they faced—and the biggest threat to their success as managers of action.

In this chapter, we look closely at some of the stark realities of resource allocation today, and see how action managers can surmount the obstacles. We focus on the resource that managers tell us they typically have to fight the hardest for—people.

Action Tips

TIP▶ Survey the Battlefield

No matter how large, how powerful, or how wealthy the organization, managers always scramble for the best people. So you, Mr. or Ms. Action Manager, need to gear up to fight for those scarce resources.

To help you survey the topography before you take to the field of battle, we have compiled a diagnostic, a series of statements. Read them carefully. If any describe your company, gird yourself for what is likely to be a protracted skirmish to secure what you need to bring your action home.

Statement: Resource allocation is more a case of the squeaky wheel getting the grease. In your company, clearly articulated, widely understood and accepted criteria don't determine priorities when it comes to resource allocation.

Statement: Your company assembles a team for a specific action, but then turns the team into an ubiquitous and permanent committee for repairing just about everything except the coffee machine and water cooler.

An organization that half-heartedly throws resources at an action will be a hard place in which to fight and win your battles.

As the first two statements in our diagnostic suggest, such an enterprise limps along, relying on an ad hoc approach rather than adopting a well-planned and orchestrated strategy to enhance its competitive position.

With no plan for the future, fairly determining what resources should be allocated to which project is impossible. If senior managers or those in control of budgets simply play favorites, they politicize action projects in ways that mystify and irritate company personnel.

As one Australian action manager lamented to us, "There are lots of priorities in our business. Unfortunately, they *all* cry out for attention."

Here are some more statements:

Statement: Your organization orders actions that cross functions or infringe on people's territories. Yet, it still parcels out resources according to function, thereby stirring up hostilities.

Statement: When your enterprise, which spends little time planning or setting strategy, undertakes a major action, it severely underestimates its capability or capacity to follow through. That is, it tries to juggle more actions than it can handle.

Statement: Permeating the organization is a sense that "time marches on—relentlessly." People seriously underestimate the time it takes to complete a project, and then start to panic when they fall behind schedule or when deadlines approach.

If any of the three preceding statements applies to your company, then it may be an enterprise characterized by arrogance and a slender knowledge of its capabilities. Inspired by extravagant proposals and visions of grandeur, many companies fall into this category, particularly if their rivals are pursuing their own agendas for competitive advantage and marketplace superiority.

An action manager in the United States surely speaks for many when she observes that, in planning a major project, "we completely underestimated the significant drain on skills."

It's a universal problem, one that plagues not just corporations, but individuals and empires, too.

At the site of the oracle at Delphi in ancient Greece, for example, an inscription proclaims: "Know Thyself." This is not an invitation to engage in something akin to modern-day psychoanalysis, but rather a warning to know what one's capabilities are and how far they extend.

Back to our statements:

Statement: Senior managers who oversee the budget misallocate resources, intentionally or not. Either they do not fully understand the nature of the action, or they have not participated in the action in the first place—and may even resent those who seek the action.

Statement: Senior managers are not convinced that the action program is all that it purports to be. They may, in fact, thoroughly distrust it or consider it a mere "add-on," a short-term fix, and not a permanent feature of the organization.

These two statements apply to you if you've yet to win over the support of senior managers. Behind both attitudes lie serious misgivings about your action program. The managers' uncertainties may inform hidden agendas and even direct sabotage, threatening the most well-intentioned action manager.

It goes without saying that if you have not yet won the full support of stakeholders, especially top managers, you cannot expect first priority when the time comes to allocate funds, people, and other resources to various projects. And if top managers view the action program as something temporary, you may win the first round of resource allocations, but find yourself fighting to justify continuing those allocations into the next quarter.

More statements:

Statement: Everyone knows who the "best" people are in the company, those dynamic and innovative go-getters who somehow finish every job they undertake. Since no good deed goes unpunished, everyone wants them on *every* team, in effect stretching them to the breaking point. There is a consensus that there are just not enough good managers to go around, and that running the business has to take precedence over implementing an action.

Statement: Your company's action programs are growing, but the number of people available to implement them is either staying the same or shrinking. Either way, there are fewer and fewer people around to pursue an action program.

The final two diagnostic statements apply to companies where there may be serious managerial problems as well as a pervasive attitude that sees certain people as linchpins in the organization.

These are essentially personnel problems—or, to be more precise, problems resulting from a lack of the right personnel. Add in the fact that organizations are attempting ever-larger makeovers, and the problems become even more pronounced. What were once departmental or site initiatives now cover the entire organization and its global operations.

In short, the issues you face in securing resources will revolve around both the quantity and the quality of those resources. In terms of personnel, there are fewer and fewer of the "best" people to help you implement bigger and bigger actions.

TIP▶ Develop a Compelling Business Case for Action

There are two reasons to construct a compelling business case for action: first, to prove that the action is necessary and will achieve its desired intentions, and second, to show that all resources will be effectively and efficiently used.

The business case presents the numbers to justify the effort and the expense of the action, but it has to do more. It must also spell out *why* you are taking this action in the first place.

To make a persuasive argument, we suggest asking yourself the following four questions:

1. How will the action support the goals of my business?
2. What specific people do I need?
3. Why should I have these people?
4. How will I deploy those people effectively?

The case for taking action becomes, in part, a selling document for convincing executives to send resources to you. But it also serves as an advertisement to entice the best people in the organization to join your team to bring the project to fruition.

You have to think like a senior executive, looking from the top down to evaluate what the business is doing, what it needs to do, and what resources are needed where.

In taking the executive perspective, you should derive a sense of how your project relates to others the organization has undertaken. You may be able to take advantage of resources dedicated elsewhere by discovering, for example, ways of bringing the best people from other projects on board.

▶

LEARN BY EXAMPLE: Bristol-Myers Squibb

One of the world's largest pharmaceutical companies, Bristol-Myers Squibb (www.bms.com), undertook a massive three- to four-year action project primarily to lower costs and meet the needs of its customers while also preparing for future growth.

Specifically, the company recognized the need to unify the business processes of its plants around the world, more closely align product supply and demand, and reduce cycle time—trials showed that, in some cases, products spent 300 to 400 days in the system, of which only 5 percent was value-adding!

Dana Cooper, leader of the demand management project, says that because of the size and complexity of the initiative, team members were recruited from a multitude of supply chains across the company and from various regions of its worldwide operations.

"We wanted a broad representation, both by region and by division, but we also wanted individuals who would be 'on loan' from their regular work," Cooper says. "This was a way of promoting the view that this was not a corporate-centric project, certainly not one relegated to the United States. It's very easy to disown the work if it's being done several thousand miles away."

◀

TIP▶ Keep Making Your Case

As the companies we surveyed can testify, action managers must continue to make the case for action to all stakeholders throughout the duration of the program.

Many of those we interviewed said that resources were most often withheld because members of the senior leadership team were never fully convinced that the action was needed or because they lost faith in the project as time dragged on. The latter situation is a problem particularly for companies engaged in marathons and decathlons.

TIP▶ Pick the Best and the Brightest

In selecting people for your action team, pay close attention to the mix of skills and personalities. Select the best and the brightest, the most creative and articulate—people who can help you build support for the action.

Include resisters if they are highly experienced and respected people who can think critically and are not afraid to speak out. Do not include them if they are merely doomsayers or sullen saboteurs.

Also identify and bring on board key stakeholders from diverse backgrounds, including geographical, functional, and cultural areas.

A word of warning: Do not accept people who have been "dealt from the bottom of the deck"—that is, those that someone else wants to get rid of.

Always keep in mind that the skills involved in designing an action are different from those required to implement it. For implementing the action, well-qualified local people are indispensable. So, by all means, include local people on your action team, and give them the autonomy to find the best way of meeting the goals set by senior managers.

Be attuned to team members' complaints and frustrations. If they say they are overworked, they undoubtedly are. After all, if you've chosen the best and the brightest in your company, how can you doubt their word?

LEARN BY EXAMPLE: Bank Corporation

With approximately $45 million in annual savings at stake, Bank Corporation set out to centralize its entire finance operation, which included 2,000 employees in approximately 40 separate business groups. Under the sponsorship of Chief Executive Officer Daniel Wright, Chief Financial Officer Aidan Burns, and Controller Jonathon Gross, the plan to reorganize the finance division and turn it into a world-class organization was developed by a core leadership team comprising the best and brightest that Bank Corporation had to offer.

But that wasn't the only criterion for selection. The members of this select group also had to be leaders within the finance division, people who had frequently spoken out on the issue at hand.

The core group was not, however, made up only of people perceived to be allies of Aidan Burns (although some were). Indeed, several people were selected because they were known to be hard resisters of the project. Viewed as much more than devil's advocates, these members were respected, creative thinkers whose intelligence and innovative ideas were highly valued.

Jonathon Gross, who participated in the interview process to select members of the core team, recalls rejecting some of the brightest people in the organization because they were perceived as not being team players.

People in a group have to recognize that they have a common task before the bonding process can begin, Gross says. Then, "so long as they receive constructive criticism, they can profit from it and not feel threatened. I interviewed a number of exceptionally bright analysts, but they had attributes to indicate they would not be good team players."

In the Bank Corporation case, the success of the action rested on the commitment of those team players and the support they received from top management.

Allocating people to such a project bears no resemblance to the playground norm of choosing the best hitters or the people with the best curve ball. Skills are important, to be sure, but you have to find people who work well together, share values (although not necessarily opinions), and are willing to put aside individual agendas in favor of what's good for the company.

If you identify and choose people with these attributes, you increase your chances for success many times over.

TIP▶ Tap Internal and External People

Action managers should search both internal and external sources for the best-qualified people. But who is best qualified depends on the various criteria you designate as critical to your action agenda.

Whether selection is made on the basis of expertise, loyalty to the company, respect of colleagues, innovative ideas, elements of diversity, or some combination of characteristics, the best-qualified people may constitute a group quite different from those who lead the company or conduct its day-to-day activities.

LEARN BY EXAMPLE: Bristol-Myers Squibb

To assure a representative mix of interests and skills, says Dana Cooper, Bristol-Myers management decided to lend people to the project team from various areas of the company, both geographical and divisional.

Theoretically, project team members worked with divided loyalties, because technically they still belonged to the divisions with which they were associated and still answered to their separate managers. In practice, however, they found camaraderie with their colleagues on the action team, and the team was able to develop a much more complete picture of the project than that available to any one unit.

In allocating human resources to this project, Bristol-Myers Squibb determined that it would be most advantageous to train a core group at its New Jersey facility. It then sent people from the group out to two pilot sites (in Greensboro, North Carolina, and Swords, Ireland), and ultimately to other manufacturing sites, where they train employees as new computer technology is installed at each plant.

In addition, at regular intervals during the planning phase, various teams of experts visited project members at the New Jersey facility to evaluate progress and determine whether the project was on track. ◄

TIP▶ Beware Half-Timers

Insist on full-time members rather than part-time people whose loyalties will be divided between serving the action and performing their regular duties. You may have to negotiate down from this position, but start out asking for more than you think you can reasonably expect.

Commitment level is clearly important, but so is who you get. The key is to get as much as you can from the right people. They may even increase their own commitment levels over time once they get involved.

Part-time involvement, however, does create management challenges.

Where part-timers are concerned, you should know that work divisions such as "50 percent normal duties and 50 percent project duties" are extremely difficult to police. Neither the manager of the project nor the managers of the various employees can keep accurate tabs on this division of labor.

Someone is bound to lose. You lose when people feel as if their loyalties are divided or in conflict. The employee loses when he or she tries to do two jobs, both at 100 percent.

This division is neither feasible nor desirable. The project suffers, and the resource allocation is stretched beyond recognition.

▶──

LEARN BY EXAMPLE: **Adaptec, Inc.**

Project manager Jim Schmidt says that management far underestimated the amount of time the company's action would take and the amount of resources it would consume. Part of the problem stemmed from the divided loyalties that people felt they owed to their normal duties or managers and to their new responsibilities as members of the action team.

For example, the Singapore facility sent 11 people to California to take part in the project. As it turned out, though, those 11 were more junior people who each called their own managers in Singapore every night to report on decisions the team was making and ask for their direction.

The need to question and seek approval extended the time frame of the first part of the project. It took several months to overcome this challenge before the onsite Singapore employees were allowed to make decisions without first consulting with their respective managers. Adaptec employees came to see the project as consuming too many resources—especially time, money, and people.

Many members of the action team itself felt that their own loyalties were divided. Vice presidents and directors from eight different areas were expected to devote 25 percent of their time to the project, but the demands of day-to-day duties meant that the requirement was seldom met—at least in the beginning stages. Later, as the critical nature of the project became apparent, more than 25 percent was required, resulting in *very* long days.

──◀

TIP▶ Quick Wins Win Resources

Projects most vulnerable to losing the battle for resources are those that seem to take forever, meandering from quarterly report to annual summary, and producing little empirical evidence that they are getting anywhere. Sooner or later, senior managers are bound to ask whether the people this kind of action uses could not be better used elsewhere.

Savvy action managers, therefore, know the importance of presenting tangible results early, just as they know to temper expectations and keep people from becoming discouraged when results do not come in immediately. As a general rule, you need tangible results no later than nine months into a decathlon or marathon. For sprints and high jumps, results need to come even faster.

Action Paths

Here's our advice on allocating resources for each of the four action paths.

▶ACTION PATH Sprint

Guarantee sufficient resources to sustain both the action program and normal customer-service levels—customers have the least patience and you have the least time.

Identify and redeploy people from noncritical business activities.

Acquire short-term experts or borrow from other areas of the company with previous action experience.

▶ACTION PATH High Jump

Recruit experienced implementers rather than concept people.

Your people have a lot to do and little time to do it in—maximize efficiency by helping them delegate line duties.

Organize task forces dedicated to specific action areas—in a merger, for example, systems integration, people selection, and organization design.

►**ACTION PATH** **Decathlon**

Pull technical people in and out as issues arise.

Plan for team modifications as your project moves through different stages.

Develop a network of long-term stakeholders and inspire them to lobby for your action when resources are allocated.

Develop an international network of skilled people to provide local support and leadership.

►**ACTION PATH** **Marathon**

Launch your action with full-time people, then streamline activities with part-time employees.

Select and recruit people with a lot of stamina, people motivated by ever-increasing performance expectations.

Rejuvenate longer-term programs with fresh resources at midpoint.

Questions and Answers

QUESTION: **What can I do when my action is competing for scarce resources with glitzy programs that have enraptured top leadership?**

You may want to reach for the first sure remedy for a headache. Contending with other managers whose projects scream just as loud for those scarce resources will make anyone's head throb.

To lessen the pain, however, you can do advance planning that will help senior managers begin to comprehend the large-scale nature of your action program and the resources it will require. Anyone who has ever dealt with home builders or home improvement contractors knows that a good rule of thumb is to take their estimates of costs and time and to add at least 50 percent more in order to get some idea of what the project will *really* cost and how much time it will consume.

That's a good rule to take with you into the planning room when you sit down with project managers to set strategy and begin constructing your arguments for allocating resources.

QUESTION: How can I get people to want to be part of the action?

Incentivize involvement. Create opportunities for people to broaden their experience, increase exposure to senior management, and fulfill some of their career goals. The objective is to generate energy and excitement so that people want to be part of the action.

5

THE THIRD CHALLENGE—
LEAD FOR ACTION

You have heard this: Lead, follow, or get out of the way.
How about: Lead and teach others to lead?
It has a more positive ring to it. It is also better business.

In his first act as king, Jean II, who ruled France from 1350 to 1364, ordered the arrest of a nobleman on charges of treason, then beheaded the man without public trial. With this one act, the king alienated the nobles whose help he would need in his country's ongoing wars with England.

Jean II is an example of what leadership is *not*. In this chapter, we define what leadership *is*—both for you, the action manager, and for others on the team and in your organization.

The need for leadership is crucial in any venture, but especially when action is required. Action makes people nervous: They could fumble their new responsibilities; they could work harder for no more pay; they could lose their jobs.

Indeed, we have seen that action can be a recipe for disaster. But with the right leadership, it can also be a formula for success. And that is where you—and we—come in.

We know of many action programs that have succeeded without strong action management. We know of far fewer that have succeeded without strong action leadership. Action management without leadership is like a car without an engine.

In our Global Action Survey, fully 82 percent of those interviewed said that "ensuring top sponsorship" was the number-one action success factor. One respondent declared, in fact, that action *is* leadership.

When we speak of the action leader, we mean that senior individual—say, a director, the chief executive officer, or a functional head—who is actively sponsoring the action. A senior team, such as the executive team or a steering group established to provide direction to the action, might be involved, too, but the team will probably still be answerable to a more senior individual.

Although we believe that, in a wider sense, all managers have an action leadership role to play, the action leader still holds a unique position: He or she is ultimately accountable for the successful delivery of the action.

We have said it before: Change is movement, movement is action, action is advantage.

This is not Pollyanna-speak. This is real.

Some leaders are born, but most need help, so we provide a model for assessing the leadership qualities of your senior executives. And, just as important, we present tips for discreetly—but affirmatively—coaching their performance.

Action Tips

TIP▶ Understand the Roles Your Leader Has to Play

Tradition dictates that a light is always left burning on stage after a performance ends and all the actors depart, after the theater is emptied out and the floors are swept in preparation for the next show.

The one light, usually a bare bulb, symbolizes the continuing life of the stage, its readiness to accommodate a new cast of actors.

In our script, as the lights go up, a newly designated action leader enters stage left, assigned to—or, possibly, the author of—this latest action drama. The role demands many different qualities—eight, to be exact.

The diagram in Figure 5.1 identifies the eight qualities that every action leader must exhibit to some degree:

1. Commit substantial time to the action.

2. Build energy, urgency, and pace.

3. Visibly support action managers.

4. Act as the vision architect.

5. Align a critical mass of stakeholders.

6. Demonstrate new values and behaviors.

7. Use symbolic actions.

8. Sustain focus and momentum.

Key Action Leadership Qualities: *Assess your action leader*

	Not observed	Sometimes observed	Frequently observed
Committing substantial time to the action			
Building energy, urgency, and pace			
Visibly supporting the action manager			
Acting as vision architect			
Aligning a critical mass of stakeholders			
Role modeling new values and behaviors			
Using symbolic actions to communicate			
Sustaining focus and momentum			

Priority areas for coaching

Figure 5.1   Action leadership qualities.

We do not consider these action leadership qualities to be a given. Sure, there will always be some whose charisma and natural gifts for inspiring others make them seem almost capable of walking on water. They have "star quality," as the song says.

But in the world in which the other 99 percent of us live—the world in which our survey respondents reside—leaders require coaching and support to develop the needed qualities.

Your action leader probably won't relish having his or her performance discussed in a group setting, though. Or, for that matter, in a private coaching session, either. Action leaders are only human, after all.

But there are a number of methods you can use. Our research turned up some informal techniques, and some that are more structured. Some involve private, one-to-one discussions between action leader and action manager; others occur as part of regular meetings.

Whatever means you use, our leadership-development techniques combined with the demands of operating in the limelight of an action program will invariably bring out the essential qualities a leader needs to deliver successful action.

TIP▶ Help Your Leader Commit Substantial Time to the Action by Influencing His or Her Schedule

Leading a complex action program consumes enormous amounts of time. How much time should your leader spend?

There is no one right answer. But 20 to 50 percent is not uncommon, depending upon the complexity of the action.

In the early stages, the time spent is determined by the level of design input required. Later, communication needs dictate the time commitment.

How can you ensure that your leader allocates the right amount of time to the right activities at the right time? One way is to take control and start booking the leader's time. Here are some ideas:

Raise the profile and exposure of your leader to the organization at large. Look for workshops or key meetings where the leader can introduce the session, contribute an item on the agenda, or simply respond to questions. Make sure other top-team members share this load.

Book time for your leader to meet with key stakeholders to discuss expectations and performance objectives. Plan periodic meetings to discuss progress.

If steering groups are used, make sure that the leader attends every meeting. Last-minute cancellations send a negative message.

▶ ─────────────────────────────────

Learn by Example: Shell Information Systems

At the extreme, the action leader can be appointed to lead the action full time. That's what happened when Clive Mather was selected to direct a major restructuring at Shell Information Services in 1995.

In that action, two large information technology functions at Shell were merged into one unit. People from both the Dutch and the English sides of the company were brought together.

Mather didn't know the people or the technology. Nor did he get bogged down in operational issues. He focused 100 percent of his time on making the action happen.

Learn by Example: The Neiman Marcus Group, Inc.

"To make an action happen, a good leader must first take the time to nurture it and support it," stresses Gerald Sampson, the president and chief operating officer of Neiman Marcus. Sampson spent no less than one day each week—a major chunk of any executive's time—spearheading his company's reengineering program.

Gerald Sampson proposed a major restructuring effort of the retail giant after he attended a seminar conducted by Michael Hammer, coauthor with James Champy of *Reengineering the Corporation.*

Inspired by the authors' enthusiasm, Sampson brought the message back home. He also invited Hammer to speak directly to Neiman Marcus employees.

"I think the leader of the reengineering effort has to make sure that the people of the organization understand how committed that leader is to it," Sampson argues.

"Here at Neiman Marcus, I did that in a variety of ways, including the speeches I gave every time I visited a store. And in each conversation I had with our employees and stakeholders, I took the opportunity to talk about the initiative."

Sampson monitored feedback, which he says "helped me to anticipate the barriers." And he also allocated time to respond to stakeholder concerns.

"One of the team leaders called me in not too long ago—they were getting into some real trouble in one particular area," Sampson says. "I took my information systems director, and we went over and let them take shots for an hour and a half over lunch. We asked about their problems, and I think we defused a lot of their concerns."

In another very visible show of support, Sampson took the entire 13-member executive group to a reengineering team implementation session. It was, he says, "another important piece in getting people up to speed and all singing the same hymn."

**TIP▶ Help Your Leader Build Energy, Urgency, and Pace
    with Prelaunch Coaching**

Your leader has to shake up the organization—rattle its cage, so to speak—by making a clear case for action and setting challenging targets. Energy and drive are indispensable qualities in this endeavor.

Urgency and pace are often determined as much by the behavior of the action leader as by the challenge of the deadlines set.

Setting the pace is particularly critical at the early launch stage. As action manager, how do you help? Keep an eye out for any event at which the action leader personally addresses senior managers and then offer to help your leader prepare.

Here are some specific points to make as you coach your leader for this appearance:

Practice with the final materials through at least two dry runs, continuing until support notes are not required. The delivery must be high energy.

Give the whole leadership team a role that demonstrates its unity.

Recognize the progress and good work of people in the room. Never disparage what has gone before.

Cover the essential points of the message—vision, values, the case for action, and the proposed result.

Deliver at least one symbolic action and link it to the urgency message.

Practice answering tough questions—remember, how you say it is just as important as what you say.

Don't make personal commitments that cannot be kept.

▶

LEARN BY EXAMPLE: British Airways Engineering

BA Engineering managing director Brian Philpott recalls his experience with setting pace: "One thing that I think I would do differently is to force the pace more. There was too much analysis. Week after week, analysis, analysis, analysis—to the extent that it became difficult to demonstrate to the world at large the progress that was being made."

The whole exercise, in Philpott's words, was "too nice and too democratic"—a sentiment that, as he acknowledges, might appear to contradict received wisdom in terms of involving and engaging people.

The reality is, Philpott declares, that "there are times when you have got to bloody well get on and do it."

◀

TIP▶ Use a Personal Contract to Ensure the Support of Your Leaders

Ever seen a senior manager hung out to dry by top leaders who withheld their support? No one is more at risk of being kicked by line management than an action manager who lacks a clear mandate from the action leader.

In the midst of the tension that surrounds an action program, key stakeholders who aren't yet committed to the action tend to direct their uncertainty and discontent toward the more junior action manager. Without the protection provided by the visible sponsorship of the leader, a manager can have a short shelf life.

What kind of support can the action manager realistically expect?

Experienced managers we know often discuss a *personal contract* with the action leader in the early stages of the action. The contract is a two-way agreement that outlines the support and behavior each person can expect from the other.

John F. Welch, Jr., chairman and chief executive officer of General Electric, expressed the underlying sentiment rather nicely: "Control your own destiny or someone else will."

That advice rings true with a U.S. project manager we interviewed whose attempt at personal contracting with his company's managing director led to a critical discovery. Here's how the manager described his experience:

> We had known each other for some time but found it useful to sit down and decide how we could best watch each other's backs dur-

ing the coming months. We talked about who we were worried most about. We even discussed what we personally hoped to get out of the process.

It was only when we talked about our respective roles that things got difficult. It became evident that my managing director was, in effect, delegating his leadership role to me.

TIP▶ Help Your Leader Shape the Vision

Today's leaders must be the architects of proposed action, drawing on finely honed instincts about what will and will not work in their own businesses and how each action fits with others.

As the overseer of the vision design, the action leader controls the breadth and depth of the action: How radical? How big? How far-reaching?

Usually, the leader establishes the central theme of the vision around which other ideas coalesce. Then, as other potential elements are identified in the vision design process, the action leader has to be convinced of each one's fit with the organization and of the underlying logic behind its selection.

The action leader, as the key shaper of the vision, can exert a considerable influence on the organization in three areas:

1. A clear vision provides strategic direction and the means to focus resources.

2. The vision becomes a natural keystone for informing everyday decisions: "Does this fit the vision?" automatically becomes the question on everyone's lips.

3. With proper communication, the vision can become a challenging motivational tool.

How can you help your action leader to act as vision architect? Try these techniques:

Get your leader involved in the design process as an active contributor to design workshops rather than as an observer awaiting the outcome for review.

Draft a summary of the vision on one page and debate it. Make sure that clear links can be made between the vision, values, and strategy.

Alert your action leader to *vision creep*—that is, the dilution and shift in emphasis and tone that occurs as senior stakeholders make their own liberal interpretations.

Test the clarity of the vision by asking: "Does it have a central theme that is easily grasped, and can it be interpreted and customized locally?"

▶
___

LEARN BY EXAMPLE: **Carlton & United Breweries, Ltd.**

From the outset, Nuno D'Aquino, the chief executive officer of the Carlton & United Breweries, clearly understood that his vision had to prepare the Australian company for tough market challenges three to four years ahead.

The vision centered around a single powerful, yet simple, theme: to shift the brewer from being more than just a market leader to becoming what D'Aquino terms a *Lead Enterprise.*

D'Aquino says he "always had this belief that Australia needed some industries to break the mold, to create a different way of working so that they could set the benchmark for other industries to follow. That's what we mean by Lead Enterprise."

The vision demanded major modifications to culture, processes and systems, structure, and working practices at Carlton. In D'Aquino's view, it was up to the action leader to start the fire.

"You can get 20-odd people together saying what do we want to do, where do we want to go, and get their input," he says. "But in the end, [the action leader] has to come out and say, 'Well, this is the way we are going to go.' "

──◀

TIP▶ Help Your Leader Win Support

The action launch is complete. Now the focus shifts to the longer process of building a critical mass of key stakeholders throughout the organization.

The challenge for the leadership is to construct an unbroken chain of influential stakeholders that starts at the top team and continues all the way through to frontline employees.

Usually, one person on the top team will join the cause immediately. Others may be more guarded. Confrontation probably won't break into the open, though, until key decisions are on the table.

Alignment may be most critical for the action leader when the team meets as a steering group to direct the action program. Norbert Gehrke, Braun personnel director, recalls how the Braun steering committee operated:

> The chairman asked everybody individually to say what they felt about the changes—not just to say yes or no, but also why. This was a very important exercise before we started. No one could argue [later], "I'm against it and I do not believe in the benefits."

Expect to bring in at least some new faces when building your critical mass of stakeholders. How many die-hard resistors will have to be replaced depends at least partly on the extent of your action.

How can you help your action leader align a critical mass of key stakeholders? Here are our suggestions:

Encourage your leader to ensure that the leadership team has the right membership and displays appropriate behaviors right at the start.

Look to build a top-to-bottom leadership chain of key stakeholders by providing your leader with a list of people to involve in the action process.

Provide opportunities to get the new leadership team in place by giving the members key roles on the action team from the outset.

Develop a top-team charter that spells out how the leadership will behave with one another and when facing the organization at large.

Network to sharpen political antennae and build the critical mass. Find good reasons for your leader to meet with people informally.

▶
_____

LEARN BY EXAMPLE: **British Airways Engineering**

At BA Engineering, action managers planned major actions that ultimately affected all 9,500 employees in over 150 locations—not just modifications in how airplanes were serviced and repaired, but also a retooling of the underlying culture of the entire organization.

As Managing Director Brian Philpott observes, building the leadership critical mass may require membership changes. "I would have thought it difficult," he says, "to bring about radical change if you have more than two-thirds of the original management still in the new world. There is too much of the old world there, and people will pull you back."

Indeed, BA made a number of new appointments during the action to strengthen the top team and middle management.

In parallel, Philpott established a network of business representatives to help build a critical mass of frontline employees. He took his leaders on walk-throughs of the repair sites, something that few people could recall ever seeing at BA.

These steps were important in convincing the unions and employees that they should take the action seriously.

Philpott perhaps regrets spending too much time getting the frontline employees on board and too little time building a critical mass of middle managers. Despite an involvement program, some middle managers still felt isolated and threatened.

The number of managers working on the action initially proved to be too few to sway their peers. The resistant managers refused even to accept that the action was serious until Philpott was able to announce a new structure and the resultant breakup of two key departments.

Although BA has continued to successfully implement the action, Philpott's experience drives home the importance of aligning a critical mass of senior, middle, and frontline employees.

◄

TIP►   Focus on the Right Behaviors and Help Your Leader Demonstrate Them

Actions, no pun intended, speak louder than words. So action leaders should demonstrate through their daily activities the values and behaviors that they want others to adopt.

Demonstrating new behaviors is not a one-shot performance. It has to be endlessly repeated, day in and day out.

To be effective, the action leader must truly believe that a specific behavior is a critical ingredient of successful business performance. Then the leader has to be prepared to challenge others to alter their behaviors accordingly.

Just paying lip service to the latest management posture won't do, either.

In our work with global clients, we see numerous instances of values allegedly being centered on customers and people, only to find action leaders who rarely meet customers and are perceived by many employees as being out of touch.

But when values and behaviors are acknowledged as the cultural blueprint for the organization, they become the bible by which your action leader lives.

How can you help your action leader demonstrate the right behaviors? Work with the leader and top team to clarify a set of values and behaviors that are central to the action (expect this to take many iterations).

Also select a few key behaviors and discuss how these can be exhibited on a daily basis by your leader—focus both on modeling the values and on ownership of the action. Finally, make line ownership of the action the first area of role modeling.

▶
LEARN BY EXAMPLE: Barclaycard

Based in the United Kingdom, Barclaycard, a division of Barclays Bank PLC, has more than 9 million credit card customers representing over 30 percent of the market in the United Kingdom. Despite its preeminent position, the company recognized that new competition posed a threat, and so embarked upon a major action program to retool its systems, operations, and culture.

Role modeling is used repeatedly at Barclaycard, both to reinforce the vision and values and to emphasize the importance of owning the action.

Linda Walton, director of operations at Barclaycard, leans back in her chair and recalls the old joke that goes: "How many psychiatrists do you need to change a light bulb?" After a pause, she says, "Only one, but the light bulb really has to want to change."

That joke largely epitomizes Walton's attitude toward action. A leader, she says, achieves results in part simply by repeating the vision at every opportunity and to as many receptive audiences as possible:

> What you've got to do is get people to see [the vision] and feel it the way you see it and feel it. You begin by living the vision today so that people can start to see what it is you are talking about for tomorrow.

Not that this is always as easy as it sounds, she observes:

Stating that you have a "no-blame" culture when nothing has gone wrong is one thing; remembering those words, and standing by them, is quite another when something has actually gone wrong.

To Walton, role modeling also means demonstrating ownership of the action. As an example, she recounts an incident that occurred just after the first stage of job selection was completed at Barclaycard.

The head of Customer Services and newly appointed managers joined with Walton to continue the selection process by choosing the supervisors who would populate the next level down. The managers complained bitterly about the entire selection process and how it had affected them.

Walton responded:

> I very much respect the fact that you had the courage to tell me how you felt. I understand the discomfort that we have put you through. However, we are now going to select the supervisors in the same way you were selected, and you will own that process. What are you going to do to make it not feel as bad for them?

Ownership is one of the first role-modeling challenges for the action leader.

TIP ▶ Help Your Leader Deliver the Right Symbolism to the Right Audience

People are sensitive to symbolism—especially if it comes from leaders:

If leaders are upbeat and enthusiastic, employees will be, too.

If leaders expect difficulties and take them in their stride, employees will react similarly.

If leaders show, through symbolism, how important the action initiative is, the rest of the organization will do the same.

Even small gestures like putting a project at the top of the agenda sends a strong signal about the need for action and the extent to which it is being taken seriously. Indeed, many of the senior people we interviewed were amazed by the power of symbolism, and had learned to use it sparingly.

One caveat on the use of symbolic gestures by the leader: This technique can be risky if the actions do not fit the corporate culture or if they unintentionally send the wrong message.

To head off unwanted consequences, the symbolism to be used should first be tested on a few trusted colleagues.

How can you help your action leader use proper symbolism? Here is our menu to help you make the right choices:

Symbolism that has a direct impact on employees: Promise a certain number of days of training per year in relation to the initiative; get rid of any symbols of the old world, such as posters, brand names, and so forth; announce changes to incentives or appraisal objectives; surprise people with new criteria for promotions that reflect the vision and values.

Symbolism that has a direct impact on senior managers: Move directors into an open-plan office; make an executive-level personnel change; eliminate signs of status, such as first-class travel.

Symbolism that has a direct impact on the action leader: Turn up unannounced at locations to view progress; promise to spend a specified number of days a week visiting sites to support the action; tell people—in fact, *promise*—what will stay the same; tell people what will happen if the action is unsuccessful.

▶ ───────────────────────────────────────

LEARN BY EXAMPLE: **The Neiman Marcus Group, Inc.**

Chief Operating Officer Gerald Sampson was keen to emphasize that Neiman Marcus's restructuring was one instance of a reengineering program targeted on growth rather than on contraction. So at the conclusion of a major speech to an annual employee meeting, a speech that was videotaped and shown to thousands of the company's employees around the United States, Sampson made a point of looking up from his notes.

In an apparently casual manner, he wondered out loud how many people had so far left the organization because of reengineering. As he did so, a screen behind him lit up with the word *zero* in eight different languages.

Sampson's symbolic action became a powerful counterforce to the fear of job losses.

--◀

TIP▶ Help Your Leader Sustain Momentum

Action is a haul, long or short, marathon or sprint.

At the outset, you are likely to find people's expectations running at full throttle. Over time, as they begin to realize how much effort they will have to put forth, their enthusiasm can sink into disinterest.

Whether it's the latest fad diet or the full-scale restructuring of an organization, human nature is clear: The toughest part of any action is finding the energy and sustaining the enthusiasm to get through the despair.

How can you help your action leader sustain momentum? Three suggestions:

1. Have your leader work with each senior manager to set personal objectives and targets that support the action.
2. Rotate new champions into the action program to rejuvenate the momentum.
3. Refuse to launch other initiatives until tangible performance results in the current initiative are being sustained.

▶--

LEARN BY EXAMPLE: British Airways Engineering

Brian Philpott introduced new life into the action program at BA Engineering by swapping key action team members. Current team members then took up critical line positions to champion the action.

Philpott also made achievement of the action objectives a high priority when setting annual personal objectives. And he heavily rationalized the portfolio of current initiatives to make space for the main action program.

The membership of the top team was continually revitalized and strengthened. In addition, the ongoing nature of the action program was communicated through the announcement of successive phases and the visible reporting of performance against targets.

As Philpott noted, there was "an unfinished job" to be done. "There is always the temptation when you are half to three-quarters of the way through to go on to the next initiative. You have to get something in there that nourishes continuous improvement."

Action Paths

Here's our advice for developing action leaders for each action path.

▶ACTION PATH   Sprint

Coach your action leader to develop a more decisive, directive leadership style. When stakes are high and time is short, people will expect to be told what to do.

Establish your action leader as the single point of accountability for the action's success.

Make sure your action leader devotes full time to the effort.

When jobs are at risk, encourage your action leader to be honest and open about it from the start. "Speak sooner rather than later" should be the guiding principle.

▶ACTION PATH   High Jump

Coach your leader to adopt a decisive, directive, hands-on style. As in the case of a sprint, when stakes are high and time is short, people will expect to be told what to do. The issue here: Problems are complex. Give people one place to go for direction.

Help your leader comprehend, and, more important, communicate, the complexity of the action.

► **Action Path**   Decathlon

Engage your action leader in reviewing and creating a short list of best practices before presenting them to the organization.

Encourage your action leader to challenge sacred cows—complex, long-term actions often require radical shifts in an organization's long-standing structure and culture.

Be prepared for leadership changes. The need to modify behaviors will not be met by all of the current leaders.

Help your leader prioritize actions into those required for the short, medium, and long term.

► **Action Path**   Marathon

Coach your action leader to serve as a role model of target values and behaviors.

Coach your action leader at regular intervals on the leadership behaviors required for the action's success.

Keep your action leader from micromanaging the action—it saps his or her energy over the long haul.

Encourage your action leader to make frequent site visits to guide implementation. Remember, in a marathon, there's time.

Help your leader develop clear performance expectations—then help him or her raise them periodically.

Questions and Answers

Question: Why do action leaders matter, anyway?

Quite simply, it all comes down to power and influence:

1. Leaders have the power to set direction and initiate action.

2. Leaders have the power to demand conformity.

3. Leaders have the power and influence to allocate resources.

4. Leaders can influence survival prospects.

QUESTION: Is leadership at the top enough?

Our survey pointed out the fact that there is often an overdependence on the top person to provide all the leadership horsepower.

Despite the trend of the 1990s to move from command-and-control to a more empowered management style, we observed that, in many instances, top management is still asked to lead the charge.

Remember that excellent action leaders share the leadership load.

QUESTION: What's the difference between running a business and leading through action?

Winston Churchill was a great wartime leader who was voted out of office in the United Kingdom's first postwar election. His constituents obviously thought Churchill's many talents were best suited to more tumultuous times—that is, leading an action rather than running a business.

In the business arena, many observers confuse the skills of running a business with those of leading an action. But, in fact, there are at least eight unique qualities of action leadership, as previously detailed, that set it apart from line leadership.

That doesn't mean, however, that the two roles are mutually exclusive. Far from it. In business today, the action leader must do both . . . at the same time.

In Australia, we interviewed more than 50 CEOs who, week in and week out, spend 15 to 20 percent of their time just focusing on increasing the capacity of their organizations for action.

QUESTION: Do perceptions of leadership vary by culture?

We believe that the influence and credibility of the action leadership is often culturally dependent. Our global survey respondents had a lot to say about their leadership, not all of it good.

Western leaders' skills come in for particular criticism. In Europe, for example, we were told at one company that "the leadership suffers from the fear of change, rather than [from] the [in]ability to implement it."

And an action manager in the United States remarked on the leadership's lack of understanding about the impact that action has on people: "While management understands why we need to change, they are far from fully comprehending the ramifications of it," he said.

By contrast, respondents in the East rated both the perceived importance of action leadership and their leaders' skills higher than did respondents in any other region.

Here, loyalty is key. As a Japanese action manager said, "It's important that we follow our leader."

Interestingly, he told us that "the arrival of a foreign leader on assignment has presented us with a dilemma. Do we continue to place loyalty with our local manager, on whose say our long-term career depends, or do we shift loyalties to our new temporary boss?"

In whatever region the action manager is based, understanding how the action leader is perceived would seem to be sound advice.

QUESTION: Do leadership qualities vary in significance over the course of an action?

Some qualities—for example, establishing a sense of urgency—will take higher precedence in the initiation and analysis phases.

Other qualities, such as sustaining momentum, become more important as the action progresses.

That is a lesson every good athletic coach can testify to. Dean Smith, a leading coach in U.S. college basketball, could drag out the final seconds of a game into several minutes, all the while exhausting his opponents as he rallied his own players with the belief that they could win.

And they did.

QUESTION: What's the difference between traditional change leadership and action leadership?

Traditional change leadership understands the importance of leadership, but leaders are unsure of exactly what they must do.

Leaders are thought to be born, not made, so their skills for change are a given. The leadership profile is patchy, and the time commitment is limited.

Finally, leadership behavior and politics are rarely discussed with the change manager.

In action leadership, on the other hand, leadership is believed to be the decisive factor. Action leaders can deliver the most critical qualities for a given action.

The leaders' skills for change are only a starting point to build upon. That's because action leaders are made, not born.

Also, line leadership and action leadership are two sides of the same coin. The action leader must do both.

The leadership profile is driven by key events, and the time commitment is high. Finally, leadership behavior is viewed as a critical ingredient and is supported through coaching.

6

THE FOURTH CHALLENGE— STRENGTHEN FOR ACTION

Middle managers aren't an endangered species about to become extinct. They are here to stay, so you had better learn to strengthen them and use them to their best advantage. Here's how.

Pity the middle managers—caught between the rock of conservative function and the hard place of looming change.

No wonder they balk at new ideas.

No wonder they are—mistakenly, we argue—seen as blockers rather than facilitators of action.

When the business action is a downsizing, they are hit hardest. When systems integration moves decision making to the frontline, the power of middle managers is diminished, and their effectiveness is weakened. No wonder they feel aggrieved.

Well, let's change our approach and bring middle managers into the action. The fruits of this approach are twofold.

First is middle managers' support of the proposed action. You gain their backing by involving them not just as foot soldiers but as participants in the design.

Middle managers are out on the floor every day. They see it all—the good, the bad, and the ugly. Their input will ensure that your action addresses reality, not just assumptions.

Second is middle managers' competent, confident, and all-out participation in implementing the action.

But for this, they need specific skills. And chances are, they don't have them. So in this chapter we show you how to teach, coach, and monitor middle managers to bring them up to speed.

You may not have an easy task, though. Middle managers are used to teaching themselves. They see "lessons" as commands from on high.

So step down from on high. Tread on their turf for a while. Introduce actions not as cost-cutting programs (with their death-knell chime of job losses) but as performance-enhancement programs that promise better and richer days for everyone.

Treat middle managers not as functionaries but as leaders in their own realm and right. Leverage their relationships with the workforce.

Easier said than done, of course. But we not only say you can do it— in this chapter, we teach you how.

Action Tips

TIP▶ Assess Middle Managers' Attitude and Aptitude

If you are looking for full approval and complete support from your middle managers, our findings show that you can expect to get it from only about 3 out of every 10.

A disturbing figure at first glance, but take heart. Although two or three out of the other seven managers may continue to openly resist your action, the rest may be receptive to suggestions and responsive to encouragement.

Before you can presume to know which middle managers might drop their guard, however, you have to assess their positions. We offer an assessment tool, shown in Figure 6.1, that helps you do just that.

Our assessment tool defines *attitude* as the manager's behavior in relation to the action. *Aptitude* is the manager's capability to lead the action locally and thrive in the new organization.

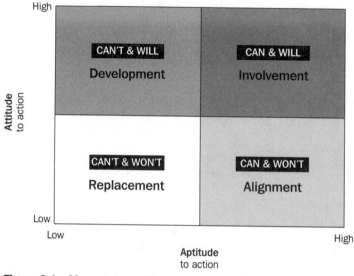

Figure 6.1 Manager's position assessment tool.

This tool can be used at key points during your action program. Although the action manager can make the assessment alone, we think it's better if the entire action team takes part. A broader perspective increases the accuracy.

Here's how the assessment grid works: You appraise each person's attitude and aptitude on an individual basis, and then place the person in the appropriate quadrant.

We developed the following role profile using nine competencies that we identified from our case-study interview feedback. Explicit in the profile are the essential attitudes and aptitudes an effective local action leader needs.

We believe that middle managers must:

1. Lead action locally.

2. Resolve resource conflicts.

3. Sustain business continuity.

4. Contribute to and challenge the vision.

5. Manage team involvement.

6. Interpret the vision.

7. Influence action horizontally.

8. Coach the team through the action.

9. Act to reassure and support.

For example, as represented in Figure 6.1, Mr. Dennis recognizes the importance of the action program, and although he doesn't necessarily see the big picture, he actively supports it.

But Mr. Dennis doesn't have the coaching, communication, and teamworking skills needed to lead his team, either through the transition or in the new organization. He thus resides in the *development* quadrant of the grid.

Ms. Ingalls, on the other hand, sees the action program as not merely an event but as a process. She recognizes the dramatic impact the proposed action will have on the organization.

Her enthusiasm is infectious, and she has quickly become a champion of the vision within her team. Ms. Ingalls resides in the *involvement* quadrant.

Mr. Allan is often described as "old world" by fellow managers.

He declines invitations to participate on key design teams where he could be an important contributor. He continues to strive for personal financial success, but at the expense of the proposed actions. He understands the need for the action, but argues for a slower, more low-key approach.

Mr. Allan resides in the *alignment* quadrant of the grid.

Ms. Repucci has consistently held her team away from the action program and is unable to recognize the need for action. She is stuck in her old ways, and doesn't have either the skills needed in the new organization or the desire to acquire them.

Unless improvement is forthcoming, Ms. Repucci resides in the *replacement* quadrant of the grid.

Here are some other suggestions:

Solicit managers' views: Ask your middle managers: What shifts have you seen in the past few years? How has your role changed? What is your perception of senior management? Of the action? How do you envision the action affecting your role? What would help you to do your job more effectively?

Tap existing appraisals: Investigate to see if you can obtain needed information through human resources or the line manager—subject, of course, to the disclosure requirements of local employment legislation.

Work with your team: Conduct the assessment as a team process, possibly including senior managers. The results are more likely to be informed and objective.

Interpret results carefully: Challenge all rationales for the placement of people on the grid. Your middle managers' true colors are evident only when you are not around.

Remember that although you may hope to find all of your middle managers in the top righthand quadrant ("Can and will take action"), a more likely figure is 50 percent. You can use the grid, however, to judge what needs to be done to move employees into that quadrant.

TIP▶ Develop Middle Managers Who Have the Attitude but Not the Aptitude for Action

What do you do with middle managers who want to take action but lack the skills? Develop them, of course.

Now, if you've ever tried to suggest to managers that they need training, you're probably thinking that we were born yesterday. We understand your skepticism.

One of our team members recalls a revealing incident that occurred recently at a British financial-services company.

Leadership training was identified as being needed to shore up the action program. But *training,* our team member was told, was for staff—managers attended *briefings* if they needed *information.*

We are well aware that the action manager also has to expect a certain degree of head-in-the-sand denial when it comes to training. But you can overcome it.

One way is to marshal strong evidence with a 360-degree feedback loop. This technique requires each manager's supervisor, peer group, and direct reports to complete a confidential questionnaire on the extent to which they observe the behaviors implicit in the role profile.

Perhaps the best action-leadership training and 360-degree-feedback deployment we have seen was at a large multinational automotive concern.

The two-day program was run several months before the action got under way. It required managers to conduct 360-degree feedback prior to attending the session.

Managers were first introduced to their roles through case studies, discussion of past action initiatives, and role-playing. Only when the managers were sufficiently comfortable with one another was the 360-degree feedback shared and discussed in pairs.

Next, the training moved towards preparing managers for specific activities: how to brief their teams on the action's vision, how to get involved in the implementation process, and how to counsel and support their teams through the transition.

Finally, each manager was instructed to prepare a development plan that had to be approved by the senior manager and incorporated into the manager's appraisal objectives. This last step assured that the good intentions would continue beyond the two-day session.

Here are some other ideas that can help you develop your middle managers:

Harness the gains made in the assessment stage by preparing development plans for your middle managers that address training, coaching, and firsthand experience needs against the role profile. Have senior managers approve personal development plans and make sure they understand their coaching role.

Use a crash training program to provide middle managers with core action leadership skills, such as communication, conflict resolution, coaching, and team building. Where time allows, broaden the scope of training to incorporate both competencies necessary for transition and competencies needed to thrive in the new organization.

Anticipate resistance to training attendance. Deploy analysis techniques such as 360-degree feedback and upward feedback from employees to provide hard evidence of gaps in the role profile.

Point out people who you believe role-model different aspects of the profile. Managers can learn by example.

For the medium term, augment the existing training curriculum for line managers to include action leadership for middle managers.

TIP▶ Involve Middle Managers Who Have the Attitude and Aptitude for Action

Humans need to feel valued. Each one of us looks for that assurance in most, if not all, aspects of our lives.

In a business environment, the extent to which a person desires to be of value to the organization often correlates directly to how well that need has been met.

This is particularly true of middle managers during the implementation of an action program. If you are to enlist this group's support and cooperation, you have to convince them that they are an integral part of the entire process.

Peter Herbert, then Barclaycard's finance and information-technology director, shared with us two interesting observations on the value of manager involvement.

First, Herbert thinks that middle managers often have "a deeper understanding" of some issues than does senior management. "Managers may be perceived as throwing up barriers or blockages," he said, "when, in fact, they are raising genuine issues and concerns that they feel need to be solved."

Herbert also noticed that managers at Barclaycard appeared to place the most value on the *process* of being consulted. "The managers were happy for the steering group to make the final decision once their views had been given," he said.

Having advanced the argument for valuing your middle managers, we must include this admonition: You cannot always involve all managers. You have to be selective.

Target those you regard as potential champions. You want to leverage their commitment. Also target those you regard as potentially negative. This group you hope to convert.

Middle managers can be included in many different ways: in full-time positions, in part-time positions, as specialist contributors, or as representatives of their functions.

Here are a few ideas:

Take a formal role in the extended action team infrastructure—as a core team member, a specialist contributor, or a business representative.

Support the development of business analyses or local interpretations of the vision, or act as an "expert" reviewer.

Manage or attend user-acceptance testing for a large system.

Attend an action leadership training program.

Take a trainer role in action program training.

Assist in the preparation of local communications.

Meet regularly with action team managers and provide input regarding program efforts.

Seek out the top 10 percent of middle managers having high potential for leadership. Select the right involvement for their skill sets. Present their example to the rest of the team and develop them as action champions.

▶
_____

LEARN BY EXAMPLE: **Iberdrola**

Iberdrola was created by a 1992 merger of Spain's two largest privately owned utilities: Hydroelectrica Española and Iberduero. Iberdrola used parallel task forces staffed with middle managers to look at specific aspects of its business. Jose Luis San Pedro, finance director, and Joaquin Ochoa, director of human resources, told us how the use of small core teams of middle managers came about.

Although a companywide transformation plan was initiated after the merger, Iberdrola's senior managers had difficulties in its implementation, due to the number and diversity of the objectives, initiatives, and teams involved. Accordingly, the transformation plan was refocused after only 15 months.

Later, the plan was reinitiated with small core teams led by Iberdrola managers and focused on specific priority areas and short-term objectives. This time, the program was successful, largely because each team received support from functional or operational directors. In addition, all operational unit managers affected by the action were involved.

The manager teams were able to implement a phased rollout that delivered benefits within short (six-month) time periods.

◀

TIP▶ Align Middle Managers Who Have the Aptitude for Action, but Lack the Attitude

Actions often start on a management high. Senior leaders are excited and inspired by the plan's anticipated benefits.

Partly because of the leaders' enthusiasm, the action plan invariably finds similar success when it is presented to senior management.

But then, when the proposed action plan cascades down into the middle tier, things begin to look a little less rosy and considerably more challenging.

What causes the change in the atmosphere?

Certainly, the middle managers have the skills they need to take action. What they may not have is the enthusiasm to make the action come to life.

It's time for alignment.

Although the term may sound somewhat sinister, *alignment* is simply about convincing your middle managers to support the action plan.

There are a number of different ways to achieve this. Most fall into the carrot-and-stick category.

The carrot of recognition and reward is difficult for most people to disregard.

When dealing with hesitant or undecided middle managers, senior managers should help them develop new performance objectives that reflect the priority of the action plan. Then, human resources should be pushed to update reward and recognition policies.

Both steps are positive ones designed to encourage the fence-sitters to come down on the side of support for the action plan.

But if the carrot doesn't entice, you may have to use the stick to propel.

Middle managers who refuse to comply with the action, and whose behavior remains inconsistent with its objectives, need to be challenged—but only by line managers. Pay attention to company procedures that may have to be followed.

After formal counseling begins, the process can either swing back, toward once again encouraging involvement in an attempt to align the middle manager, or forward, toward the last resort of replacement.

Here are a few other pointers for aligning middle managers:

Anticipate varied reactions. You will rarely encounter managers who react only positively to the action program.

Plan for support, indifference, and resistance, and handle each reaction appropriately. Delegate issues to line managers—stay out of the firing line.

Change the personal objectives of middle managers to reflect the proposed changes in the action plan. Understand the significance of recognition; the right amount of encouragement from the action leader is often worth more than monetary rewards.

Educate all senior management as to why middle managers resist action. Provide them with a portfolio of useful techniques, such as those used at Braun.

▶───

LEARN BY EXAMPLE: **Braun**

Managers at Braun, the global consumer-products manufacturer, ensured manager alignment from the outset of the action program by setting expectations early.

Dieter Timmermann, the company's chief financial officer, told us that "one of the ground rules for managers was that they *not* start by asking, 'How will the project impact me?' " Braun "recognized that managers may have hidden agendas around turf protection, but that conflict can be avoided if they concentrate on processes first."

Any resistance from managers toward the proposals, Timmermann went on, was then dealt with from the top down.

◀

TIP▶ Replace Middle Managers Who Have Neither the Attitude nor the Aptitude for Action

We were recently intrigued by a managing director's presentation to automotive company middle managers at the beginning of an action program. He described what he called "the last 10 minutes of the movie"—his vision for the company.

"Everyone here must decide for themselves if they wish to be in the last 10 minutes," he said. "There will be places for those who do and can step up to the standard. I imagine there will also be those who will not. *You* must decide where you are going to be."

In an action of any significant size, the reactions of managers are never casebook perfect.

No matter how conclusively the need for action is demonstrated, there will always be dissenters.

No matter how clearly the action processes are communicated, there will always be middle managers who are incapable of carrying out the required work.

Either they are unwilling to support the action or they are unable to implement it. Either their attitudes fall short or their skills don't measure up.

As we said before, you can expect unequivocal support from only about 30 percent of middle managers. Most of the rest will be undecided. They will need to be convinced and encouraged.

But a small percentage will never back the action. When you are sure they won't budge, rotate them to another area or replace them altogether. And do it quickly, before these naysayers can influence colleagues and those under their leadership.

Remember, the right middle-management behavior is critical to securing any action with a cultural shift. If you cannot change the behavior, you have to change the people.

Situations like this are regrettable but not uncommon. Action is extremely difficult for most people. Not everyone is up to the task.

On the bright side, accepting this reality is half the battle.

The challenge for the action manager then is to recognize trouble spots early through effective assessment of middle managers. When replacement is the only option, time is of the essence. Otherwise, reluctant or openly defiant managers can become a thorn in the side of the entire project.

▶ ───────────────────────────────

LEARN BY EXAMPLE: SkyChefs, Inc.

Caterer to many of the world's best-known airlines, Dallas-based Sky-Chefs, Inc. acquired a financially strapped Caterair and its nearly 25,000 employees in 1995. Chief Executive Officer Michael Kay had a clear vision to dramatically improve performance in the company's kitchens by cutting the time needed for food preparation and distribution to aircraft.

But after some initial work to introduce its cycle-time-reduction program, SkyChefs found itself struggling with managers who lacked both the aptitude and the attitude for the action.

As Steve Skogland, vice president for the CTR project, told us, "We started doing some assessments on the ability of the managers and supervisors to manage the process change. We decided to spend a whole day talking in a very simplistic way about core competencies of the organization. That's when we first came to the revelation that we had a huge gap in the existing organizations and their capability of driving action."

Kay's vision of "having kitchens worldwide that use cycle time as a driver of performance" was threatened—by costly delay if not outright collapse.

What did SkyChefs do?

"We stopped the deployment," Skogland said. Then, SkyChefs brought "a very seasoned senior operating executive from the States to Europe to help drive the process, and we established a profile of what managers and supervisors needed to look like in Europe."

◀

Action Paths

Here's our advice on strengthening middle managers for each action path.

▶**ACTION PATH** **Sprint**

Set and monitor short-term performance targets for each middle manager.

Watch for rising stars among middle managers—and bring them on board quickly.

Focus on middle managers with a reputation for moving quickly.

▶**ACTION PATH** **High Jump**

Assign recalcitrant middle managers to task forces with strong leaders.

Put supportive middle managers in critical positions early in the program.

Establish and communicate how layoffs will be handled before any middle managers actually lose their jobs.

Be prepared to deal decisively and swiftly with resisters.

▶**ACTION PATH**   **Decathlon**

Run middle-management workshop programs to generate ideas and support over the long haul.

Encourage reluctant middle managers to seek inspiration and assistance both inside and outside the organization.

Make middle managers accountable for local action.

Involve middle managers in building the business case for action from the bottom up. Make sure contributions are specifically acknowledged.

▶**ACTION PATH**   **Marathon**

Design and implement long-term middle-manager training and development programs, using individual modules for each key element of the action.

Monitor and test middle managers' behaviors with 360-degree feedback programs.

Rotate middle managers through various jobs during the action's duration.

Integrate the action-performance measures for middle managers into the organization's human-resources policies.

Questions and Answers

QUESTION: Why do middle managers resist action?

As with many situations in life, the actual problem is cloaked in a multitude of accompanying perceptions. But our personal experience within numerous organizations, and the results of our Global Action Survey, reveal a number of insights into the dilemma of middle management.

Here is what we learned:

1. Recalcitrant middle managers are cited as barriers to action three times more frequently than are ineffective leaders.

2. Middle managers often act as a glass floor to the downward cascade of action programs. The problem is particularly acute with actions that emphasize behavioral or cultural shifts.

3. Forty-nine percent of major action programs lack the proper management skills at the middle-management level. Almost half! We believe the shortfall has two root causes: lack of clarity of the middle-manager action-leadership role and low commitment to the development activities required to underpin it.

4. Middle-manager resistance occurs in the formative stages of an action program, but peaks as implementation approaches—when the impact is most catastrophic.

5. Many actions cut disproportionately into the manager tier. Yet, in interviews with more than 100 middle managers across Europe and the United States, we found surprisingly high levels of job satisfaction. Why? It seems many managers are happy where they are. They have already achieved their career goals. Not everyone wants to be chief executive officer. The stress and pressure of senior management does not appeal to every manager. The middle is exactly where they want to be.

QUESTION: How do development, involvement, alignment, and replacement differ from stakeholder management?

Stakeholder management traditionally puts too much focus on merely identifying and challenging opposition. Our approach presents a more positive agenda that objectively assesses the attitude and aptitude of middle managers, then matches them to the right strategy to support improvement.

QUESTION: Aren't middle managers a thing of the past?

Tom Peters, who claimed that "middle management . . . doesn't just slow our organizations down. It moves them backward . . . [and] clogs our corporate arteries" would have you believe they are. We disagree. As you learn to treat your middle managers not as mere functionaries, but as leaders in their own realm, you will harness their participation in implementing your action plan. By training middle managers in the skills required to manage an action, you will avoid the glass floor problem.

This is what occurs when action programs arrive at a managerial level that is unskilled and uncomfortable with the complexity of these programs—from there on down, the implementation of necessary steps is constrained. And finally, by valuing the input of your middle managers, you will ensure that your action addresses reality rather than mere assumptions.

CHAPTER

7

THE FIFTH CHALLENGE— MOBILIZE FOR ACTION

Involve employees? So what else is new? Though the idea isn't new, the practice of doing it is still poorly mapped territory. With this chapter, we draw you a full map.

The word *mobilize* conjures up images of war.

Battalions boarding troopships. Tanks roaring across scarred battle-grounds. Flight-suited pilots in the ready room as the order comes to "Scramble!"

Well, an action program *is* war.

It is a war against outmoded practices, competitive pressures, and the clock.

What it should *not* be is war within the ranks.

Yet, sometimes it is.

We all want to feel secure. But action shakes us up. We all want to be valued for the work we do. But action destabilizes our personal currency.

Action is good unless it is in our backyard.

So what do employees do when action threatens them? They resist.

At the outset of an action program, you might expect that roughly 30 percent of your employees will support the action enthusiastically. Another 20 percent will oppose it no matter how much they are prodded, pampered, and pacified. The remaining 50 percent will waver from yes to no and no to yes well into the action's implementation.

Resistance will diminish only when employees have lived with the action long enough to personalize it, improve it, and *own* it.

But it isn't necessary for all employees to support an action for it to succeed. Many action programs successfully proceed with varying degrees of employee buy-in.

We believe that you need only a *critical mass*—about half of all employees—to implement an action. The rest will follow in their own good time.

Your job, then, is to manage resistance.

That is what this chapter helps you do.

Trying to lure them with exhortations may just drive them further away.

Consider their resistance as energy, although in a negative form. Harness that energy. Flip it around. Turn AC power into DC—alternating current into direct, supportive effort.

Your people want and need to get involved—designing and implementing action, setting targets, measuring accomplishment, and establishing scales of compensation. You must recognize and deal with them as individuals, work units, and unions.

Then, you must unite these diverse segments in the common cause upon which you all agree: reaching peak business performance. Here's how.

Action Tips

Tip▶ Understand Why Employees Resist

Employee resistance can come from any level of the organization, wherever fear, rumor, or misinformation run unchecked. It is fueled by poor communication.

In fact, when it comes to resistance to an action program, it is impossible to overstate the importance of communication. To be successful, action management *must* include a two-way dialogue between employee and employer.

Our rule of thumb, which has been proven time and again: *The less communication, the more resistance.*

To illuminate the point, consider the following entries from a diary detailing a mythical midlevel employee's responses to a major action.

> *Day 1:* Pretty much the same old same old around here. In at 9, out by 5. Fine by me—leaves me plenty of time to work in my garden and surf the Internet. The company doesn't ask for the sun and the moon, and I don't offer it. But, hey, neither does my boss.
>
> Heard some grumbling today about the competition, how they're delivering better service than we are. The same stuff trickles down every year from the big shots, just before they announce job cuts. I'm not worried. I've got 20 years under my belt. Besides, when the company tried to make changes two years ago, it was a complete disaster. Nobody told us what was going on or asked for our input. The managers constantly contradicted themselves, the CEO was off at some meeting in Asia, and the whole shebang was sprung on us out of the blue. It fizzled out and nothing changed. Not that I'm complaining.
>
> Actually, I do have a few ideas for sharpening up our service end, but, hey, nobody seems to be too interested in hearing them.
>
> *Day 2:* I'm in shock. The big shots called us all together today in the auditorium and the CEO stood up and announced a major new "vision" for the company. Sounded to me like the main component was "rightsizing"—layoffs, in plain English. Why the hell can't management talk to us like adults?
>
> I left the meeting feeling wiped out and empty. No one around here feels like working. How could they do this to us? There was no

warning. After the meeting, our supervisor asked everybody on our team to talk about the change. People were too demoralized to say much. I felt like saying: "You're the supervisor, you explain it." Nobody seems to know what's happening.

Day 10: Today, we all were invited to a workshop to find out more about the changes. A total waste of time, no doubt. But maybe I'll at least get a chance to offer some of my ideas. Is that too much to hope for?

Day 11: The meeting went pretty well. My team members and I decided to be completely honest. We really let the managers know how we felt. Reminded them about the last time they tried to change things—how they didn't involve us, kept us in the dark the whole time, treated us like we were expendable. The good news is that we left the meeting with a sense that they actually listened to us for the first time.

Day 100: Looks like another big fizzle, another stupendous waste of time. It's been three months and nothing much has changed. We haven't heard anything in a while. Of course, we're always the last to know. Maybe the project's on hold; maybe the managers changed their minds. My boss spends a lot of time in meetings and workshops. Don't ask me what they're about.

Day 150: The company is still making a half-assed attempt to change things. But guess what? My boss doesn't even believe in it. Yesterday, I was invited to a meeting to review the new information-systems design, and my boss said, "Don't sweat it. Other people will be there. Let's not give these changes any more help than we absolutely have to!" Boy, talk about getting mixed signals.

Day 170: A letter arrived in my mail yesterday: "Dear Mr. Eldredge, we are pleased to invite you to discuss a new job opportunity here at Smithers Corporation." Great. Now they want to take my job away. The whole damn thing is their fault in the first place. If they would just run the company with half a brain and use all their fancy computers, our service division wouldn't be lagging to begin with.

Spent all afternoon staring at the computer screen. I feel let down, unmotivated, angry. Couldn't sleep last night—got up at 3 A.M., logged on, and did some surfing.

Day 250: After almost three months of doing virtually nothing, they're suddenly screaming about training. Training? Why does somebody my age have to go through training again? Three days of "orientation and reskilling," according to the materials. All I want is some straight answers to straight questions—about MY job. I'm going to give those trainers hell. I'm angry and really stressed out.

Day 300: We went live today, or rather the new ERP system went live. The place was chaotic—papers and desks being moved, phones ringing, angry customers trying to find someone to listen to them. A "welcome to the new world" letter was placed on our desks sometime during the night. Unfortunately, the training I got for the "new world" was totally inadequate. I'm floundering, and so are most of the people I work with. We're very short of people.

Day 370: Yesterday, I realized we've been on the new system for over two months, and I still feel like I've been pushed off the deep end and told to swim. So I made a decision. If it's the last thing I do, I'll figure out how to do this job and do it well.

I took the paperwork home last night and worked late on my own computer. Today, I managed to do three correct entries on the new system back to back. What a great feeling! Plus, I was able to help Joan and Wallace get the hang of things. I think I'll write up a few suggestions and give them to my manager. He asked me if I would, and, damn it, I'm going to take him up on his offer. See if he really means it.

Day 400: Picking up the pieces. The last month hasn't been pretty. The big resisters are gone. They included some of our best, and worst, people. A lot of them were my friends. I feel guilty that I was chosen to stay. But I worked hard to earn it.

Service complaints are way down and the company has actually incorporated a few of my suggestions. The people on my team are tired, though, and it seems like there's a never-ending stream of new initiatives that put new pressure on us. All I want is some stability, a chance to settle down and get used to these changes. Some days I get home too tired to do anything but eat dinner and sack out.

Day 440: I got my first "post-live" appraisal today. Not bad. The company recognized the contributions I've made, and the new responsibilities I've taken on. There were some suggestions for improving my performance on the new software. It's been over a year since all this started—some days it seems like five—but I'm starting to feel really good about the work I'm doing.

The company seems to have learned some valuable lessons, too. Most important, they appear to be actually listening to our thoughts and suggestions, not just asking for them.

Like most of us, the author of our imaginary diary prefers the stability of the tried-and-true ways of working to the uncertainties of an action program.

He exhibits all the predictable fear and misgivings, and he resists by declaring that he is going to give managers hell. He angrily rejects the notion of training. He feels guilty when coworkers are asked to leave while he is chosen to stay.

Once he begins to accept the action and assume added responsibilities, he comes to defend the program. That response demonstrates the power of buy-in from employees who, as he puts it, have been "invited" to offer suggestions on the action's progress.

By the time the diary closes, our mythical employee has not only made the transition but is also *mobilized* to see the project through to completion.

Action, as our diary shows, can be a bitter pill for some employees. You, as action manager, must help them swallow it by providing outlets for them to quickly—and constructively—channel anger and frustration.

TIP▶ Hold Action-Readiness Workshops

You know some employees will resist, so what are you, Mr. or Ms. Action Manager, going to do?

Your first step is to assess the level of resistance.

Here's how: Hold employee sessions to identify and address issues related to the action. We call these *action-readiness workshops.*

Workshops are a low-risk way of initiating employee involvement and presenting a positive face of the action program.

Many respondents to our Global Action Survey reported success with such workshops. A German manager at one multinational corporation told us that "workshops were extremely valuable in involving employees." He went on to explain:

> A lot of people work late shifts, and tend to feel unnoticed. They work odd hours: It's a different culture. . . .
>
> Even when you ask people to talk to you if they have any problems, they never do it—even though these are the same people who complain the loudest that they haven't any control over their own destiny!
>
> We realized that we couldn't go forward if significant groups felt that way, so we put together some focus groups to help bridge those gaps.

What do you need to know about action-readiness workshops?

First of all, invite at least 10 percent of the employees affected by the action.

Workshops for frontline employees typically run two hours, certainly no more than four, and may involve any number of employees.

When your workshops are completed, then what?

Repeating workshops within different functions and on different levels of the organization helps to map employee resistance. We advise separate workshops for managers, whose involvement is likely to differ both in kind and in degree from that of frontline employees.

A reminder: You can tackle resistance only when you know where it is.

TIP▶ Spot Potential Resistance

How ready is your company to implement an action if it were to start today? That is the question you seek to answer here.

We developed a readiness assessment tool for use in action-readiness workshops. We suggest that you ask each workshop participant to complete the questionnaire. Then you should consolidate the results and summarize them for the group, perhaps using a flip chart. (See Figure 7.1.)

More advice: Highlight and discuss any large gaps between perceptions of your organization's current situation and what's required for your action program. Ask participants to explain their answers.

Workshop participants quickly get used to expressing themselves, so invite them to answer these questions in person:

What thought, comment, or question is of most concern or importance to you as an employee?

What would you like to tell or ask managers?

Please assess how our organization stands *currently*. Then repeat the assessment for how it is *required* to be in order to deliver the changes.

	Slow pace	**Current**		**Required**	Fast pace	
Pace of work	Current	1	2	3	4	5	6
	Required	1	2	3	4	5	6
	Too many					*Too few*
Initiative level	Current	1	2	3	4	5	6
	Required	1	2	3	4	5	6
	Distrusted					*Respected*
Leadership	Current	1	2	3	4	5	6
	Required	1	2	3	4	5	6
	Drives decisions & behavior					*Unimportant to decisions/behavior*
Hierarchy	Current	1	2	3	4	5	6
	Required	1	2	3	4	5	6
	Heavily resisted					*Quickly embraced*
Change	Current	1	2	3	4	5	6
	Required	1	2	3	4	5	6
	Limited, need-to-know basis					*Open & direct*
Communications	Current	1	2	3	4	5	6
	Required	1	2	3	4	5	6
	High morale & job satisfaction					*Low morale & job satisfaction*
People	Current	1	2	3	4	5	6
	Required	1	2	3	4	5	6
	Protect turf					*Actively work cross-functionally*
Internal boundaries	Current	1	2	3	4	5	6
	Required	1	2	3	4	5	6
	Limited use & familiarity					*Central to our work*
Technology use	Current	1	2	3	4	5	6
	Required	1	2	3	4	5	6
	Happy as we are					*Strive for large improvements*
Performance	Current	1	2	3	4	5	6
	Required	1	2	3	4	5	6

Figure 7.1   Action readiness assessment tool.

What would make you feel more personally committed to the action?

With these questions, you begin to identify and confront the hot buttons that must be addressed later in your communication program.

Again, summarize the answers on a flip chart. Group and prioritize similar issues for discussion.

Don't be surprised by what you hear. In our experience, the most common issues are grounded in fear about an action's impact.

TIP▶ Past Resistance Is a Guide to Current Resistance

You need to understand the factors that were critical to the success of your previous actions. You also need to know where resistance was encountered.

We suggest you invite participants to identify successful and unsuccessful actions. Then ask them to say why some failed while others succeeded. Be sure to pinpoint specific areas of employee resistance and difficulty by asking such questions as the following:

Did people lack the skills the action required?

Were they adequately compensated for the new work they were asked to perform?

Did they understand why some jobs were lost?

Did they believe the company treated employees fairly?

TIP▶ Defuse Resistance with Involvement

The key to battling employee resistance is *employee involvement*. A program to involve employees can help in three ways:

1. You can use each event as an opportunity to communicate with employees. And you already know the importance of communication.

2. Employees often know more about the minutiae of a business's processes than management does. The wise action manager knows that the simple process of exposing rough plans to employee scrutiny will produce much of the needed refinement. It isn't criticism. It's valuable local feedback.

3. Involvement makes people more positive about the whole process. Vague uncertainties about the future begin to be replaced with more concrete glimpses of how the plan might work in practice.

There is a catch to employee involvement, though: It costs time and money, and it can often lengthen the duration of an action. Few, if any, companies can afford to involve everyone all the time.

Involvement also sets up the expectation that individual contributions will be acted upon. In fact, only a few can be implemented. Make this point clear to participants to head off potential disillusionment.

There's still another catch: Involvement doesn't fit all national cultures.

In our Global Action Survey, we observed significant regional differences. For example, twice as many companies in the United States and Europe considered involvement critical as compared to their Far Eastern counterparts.

So how do you involve employees and reduce resistance? Here's our checklist.

1. Solicit Feedback

Various techniques, such as employee or communication surveys, focus groups, interviews, and action readiness workshops, allow you to involve a significant number of employees in your action program.

At one European utility we visited, the results of a 25,000-employee survey were the impetus for an initiative to retool the company culture. The responses spurred management to act.

The chief executive officer launched the action program when he detailed the results to employees and outlined a program of action to address the issues that were raised.

2. Solicit Ideas

Solicitations often take the form of an invitation to a workshop program that is designed to cover as many employees as possible.

BA Engineering, for example, conducted an extensive program of so-called envisioning workshops that reached more than 1,000 employees.

Each workshop lasted two to three hours and covered ideas that could be introduced quickly, followed by opportunities for more radical improvements. The action team coalesced ideas around key common themes, then presented them to managers for further development.

3. Invite Team Participation

In Chapter 5, we suggested that, ideally, people will participate on an action team as full-time core team members, but that it may be appropriate to have part-time involvement from some individuals.

Perhaps the best examples of involvement are found at companies that actually build participation into the core jobs of all employees. One such approach is the use of suggestion programs.

An aerospace company we visited encourages employees to submit innovative ideas to managers using a standard format. Ideas are screened, then forwarded to a local review panel, which examines their value and feasibility.

Accepted ideas are rewarded with prizes on a sliding scale that reflects the value of the idea to the company. Outstanding ideas and their originators receive high-profile recognition from the chief executive.

Another example of strong day-to-day involvement is found at Kawasaki Heavy Industries, Ltd. There, employee teams meet every morning to discuss how to improve performance. Only modest action- and training-team involvement is required to ensure consistent use of the improvement methods and tools.

4. *Measure the Extent of Involvement*

Monitor statistics on the number of interviews conducted, workshops held, progress reviews accomplished, and so on.

Set coverage targets and determine how many people should be invited to participate in the various activities. Aim to involve at least 10 to 20 percent of employees.

5. *Carefully Select Those You Involve*

The employees you select should be visionary, influential, and likely to use their influence to persuade others.

Be sure to actively involve key dissidents and vocal employee leaders. Otherwise, they may adversely affect your action.

6. *Be Forthright*

As soon as you can responsibly do so, disseminate information about job cuts, new assignments, and retraining. Hiding or delaying information—or, worse yet, lying about it—will get you into trouble with employees. And, ultimately, the company's credibility will be undermined.

7. *Explain Standards*

At the outset, detail the standards that dictate how people can expect to be treated.

Explain how and when the standards will come into play, and how and when decisions that affect job content will be made.

Document these standards in writing.

8. *Train Line Managers*

It is critical to provide line managers with the coaching and counseling skills that will enable them to support employees in transition.

9. *Support Work Teams*

Make it clear to line managers that they are responsible for supporting each and every member of their work teams.

10. *Involve Unions and Work Councils*

Inform, consult, and negotiate with the unions and work councils as a body. But involve their representatives as employees—they can be powerful agents for action.

Also discuss with these groups how to treat their members fairly.

▶ ───

LEARN BY EXAMPLE: **Carlton & United Breweries, Ltd.**

Nuno D'Aquino, chief executive officer of Carlton & United, freely admits that, in a previous action, his program for involving employees wasn't completely successful.

"The company ran workshops all over Australia," he says, "involving hundreds of people—factory people, salespeople, drivers, the whole lot."

Although employees seemed highly motivated at the conclusion of the workshops, managers belatedly discovered that much of the talk had been about changing beliefs, rather than about changing business processes, systems, and behaviors.

So the action began to unravel.

"Within two weeks," D'Aquino notes, "most of the motivation was gone. And within three weeks, we found ourselves in trouble because we had created a promise without being able to deliver anything tangible quickly enough to keep people's interest."

This time around, D'Aquino enlisted the help of a senior Carlton & United management team that included Alan Kemp, vice president for human resources, and Rick Beker, vice president of lead enterprise strategies. Keeping his previous experience in mind, D'Aquino initiated a two-stage process that slowly worked its way through management and then to all employees.

In the first stage, notes Kemp, "We committed the organization to a process of conditioning, whereby people discovered the vision and the culture, and the attributes that were needed to support that vision and culture. There was nothing imposed. I think the most important thing in the process was that most people went away saying it was a journey of self-discovery."

Carlton & United's pace was initially conservative, so involving 300 to 400 people in 20 workshops took longer than some people might have liked. Once the groundwork was laid, though, Carlton & United shifted gears and extended the involvement of employees in three areas.

"First, we covered 60 workshops and 1,000 people in 18 months," says Kemp. "Second, Carlton & United initiated the design and implementation of a large *Genesis* information system replacement with wide cross-functional employee involvement. Third, the pace was additionally driven by the introduction of 20 concept teams, each responsible for one aspect of enterprise leadership."

D'Aquino describes the concept teams as groups of people "from many disciplines who take an idea (the concept) articulated by action leaders and brainstorm how they can bring it to life." The chief concept team, which reports directly to D'Aquino, may assign parts of complex actions to subordinate concept teams throughout the organization.

D'Aquino says he held to one key involvement principle throughout: "Nobody was relieved of their current roles. Everybody who was on the concept team also had a normal job."

According to Beker's estimates, up to 70 percent of Carlton & United employees were involved, directly or indirectly, in at least one of the three activities.

Interestingly, this high degree of involvement and support came from the most self-confident and self-reliant employees, not the youngest or newest to the staff who were just beginning to assimilate the corporate culture.

◀

Action Paths

Here's our advice on mobilizing for each action path.

►ACTION PATH Sprint

Focus all communication on excitement and speed of payoff.

Rapidly deflect or accept blame when employees target you instead of assuming collective responsibility for improvement or failure.

Offer generous, time-based incentives.

Give people frequent opportunities to express their feelings and air their grievances—there's no time to hold back.

►ACTION PATH High Jump

Let employees know that short timetables mean restricted consultation on planning and implementation activities.

Set up a central clearing house for action updates and information.

Plan to communicate with a diverse audience about diverse issues— when complexity is high and deadlines are tight, nearly everyone needs, and deserves, a different answer.

Deliver action-related news—good and bad—honestly and quickly.

Keep everyone focused on key events and milestones—resistance rises when details distract.

►ACTION PATH Decathlon

Keep employees reaching ever higher. Preempt resistance by appealing to their pride in past achievements, then pump them up for the next event.

Take ample time to ensure that employees understand the vision and implications of the action—in a decathlon, preparation is crucial.

Allow for local customization—but not frequent debate or negotiation.

Take time to get the right people in place—don't compromise; poorly placed employees are a prime source of resistance.

▶**ACTION PATH   Marathon**

Survey employees before project launch, then every six to nine months thereafter, about current values and behaviors introduced.

Facilitate shared norms—and reduce resistance—by soliciting confidential upward feedback.

Celebrate milestones, and progress in between.

Periodically realign employee-performance measures.

Questions and Answers

QUESTION: How common is employee resistance?

Employee resistance is the norm. Indeed, one in three of the companies we surveyed reported employee resistance as a major challenge.

QUESTION: What's the root cause of employee resistance?

Several action managers identified fear. All of us, of course, tend to fear what we don't know, understand, or control.

When an action program threatens jobs—whether that threat is real or perceived—employees often circle the wagons to protect what they believe to be their best interests. Who can blame them?

QUESTION: Is employee resistance a consequence of bad management?

No, it is an integral part of the action journey. And if it is managed with understanding and empathy, employee resistance can become a positive opportunity for personal and organizational growth.

QUESTION: What is the best way to plan for employee resistance?

By addressing it in *all* agendas at *all* levels at *all* times.

A common mistake is to underestimate the intensity of resistance to action. Many of the action managers we interviewed admitted they were surprised by the fervor of the opposition.

"Don't underestimate the impact change can have on staff morale," one manager cautioned. "I did, and it cost me dearly in time, energy, and resources."

Another said, "There was an assumption by senior management that change was going to go through without any employee resistance. In hindsight, we were incredibly naïve."

We believe that methods of countering employee resistance should be built into the planning and implementation stages of an action program, then continuously assessed and revisited as the action unfolds.

One thing is clear: Ignore resistance at your peril.

QUESTION: What can be done to protect employee interests during the planning and implementation of an action?

Few things send a stronger signal than the publication of a code by which employees can expect to be treated. We call it an *employee charter,* and it can define and resolve many of those issues that, if left unanswered, will rapidly increase employee resistance.

The finance department of a major U.S. high-technology company provides an estimable example.

This organization published a one-page charter setting out how new jobs would be defined and advertised, and how appointments would be made. It also specified how managers would be expected to behave, and how employees would be involved in key decisions affecting their areas. Finally, it spelled out what support and advice would be available.

QUESTION: What are the key skills needed by managers as they guide employees through an action?

Action creates stress throughout an organization, and managers often need training to perform successfully. That training should include the building of interpersonal skills such as coaching and counseling.

Remember: Managers are human, too, and may need hand-holding from *their* superiors during the action program.

QUESTION: What's the best way to involve unions?

Our experience shows that the path of least resistance is to include unions in the action program from the start.

Unions can play a critical role in shaping both the initial terms of the charter that protects employees during the action program and the final terms that apply when the program is complete. We strongly advise that communications start early and that it be conducted in an open and trusting manner.

Remember: No two unions or work councils are the same. A union's behavior is governed by its history and tradition, prevailing culture, competitive context, existing agreements, and so forth.

Understand the workings of each union you will be dealing with *before* you begin negotiating the specifics of your action.

When the Spanish utility Iberdrola instituted a series of major actions after its 1992 merger, a key component of the action program called for a 30 percent reduction in personnel—to 10,700 employees from 16,000 by the year 2000.

The presence of seven employee unions, each with differing priorities, complicated the goal. But Iberdrola action managers managed to elicit support by promising to create 150 new jobs a year for 5 years.

All the terms and conditions were negotiated under what was known as the collective agreement. In addition, the unions and the company agreed to a policy of no compulsory redundancies and no reductions in individual salaries and benefits.

Such steps sent a clear signal that Iberdrola was determined to treat everyone fairly. As a consequence, Iberdrola has been able to work with the unions not only to reduce its workforce, but also to redefine existing positions so as to emphasize flexibility and multiple skills.

Joaquin Ochoa, director of human resources, estimates that the company has reduced the number of different jobs from the prior 2,500 to the current 300 to 350 "families" of jobs.

QUESTION: Are there any special challenges for dealing with employee resistance in different cultures?

Every country presents its own specific challenges, and managers must never attempt a one-size-fits-all action program.

In Japan, for instance, employee resistance takes a different, less obvious form, because of the Japanese business culture. Japanese companies prefer to work through a complex network of consensus. Leaders will not proceed until they are satisfied that they have the full support of their colleagues and employees.

Indeed, the process of consultation can be extensive and far lengthier than in many Western companies. This process is known as *nemawashi*—which, incidentally, is translated as "root-binding."

Nemawashi has some similarities to the Western process of obtaining buy-in. But it is fundamentally different in that confrontation is rare and the resistance of even one employee carries much more weight.

Although *nemawashi* can try the patience of Western managers, any delays are preferable to the disruption and loss of morale caused by attempting to impose tactics that don't respect Japanese culture and customs. Indeed, the delays caused by *nemawashi* are often recovered once the decision to go forward is reached and the entire organization takes action.

8

THE SIXTH CHALLENGE—
CLARIFY FOR ACTION

Communication does more than just transfer information.
It kindles passion—not the warm, fuzzy kind,
but the kind that ignites action.

In a contemporary play, several innocent men are questioned about a robbery. One explains why they should tell the truth: "It's the easiest thing to remember."

When communicating information about your business action, you should tell the truth because anything less will cause you to lose the trust of your employees.

And without that trust, as well as the clarity of communication that underlies it, you will have a tough time getting people to invest their minds, hearts, and souls in the project.

The next thing you know, you will be trying to make do with a delayed or partial implementation of your action—that is, if there is any implementation at all.

Why risk setting this destructive cycle in motion?

Good communication has two parts: It tells people *what* they should do, and it tells them *why* they should do it. This chapter offers techniques and tactics for communicating both.

You will see how good communication engenders the kind of commitment that best serves business action, and best promotes the interests of the organization and the individuals from which it comes.

Also, you will discover how effective communication and canny media choices can spark interest, sustain enthusiasm, and drive an action to a successful conclusion.

Sustaining enthusiasm is vital, especially in lengthy projects. People get bored, anxious, and distracted waiting for promised results.

Incessant, repetitive communication will only drive them further away. Too little communication will send the project off their radar screens entirely.

But a happy medium of well-timed and focused messages will recharge low batteries and keep the action on track. Here's how.

We have identified—and illustrated in the diagram in Figure 8.1— four communication priorities that affect every action. As we noted in Chapter 1, an action moves through the five stages of (1) initiation, (2) analysis, (3) definition, (4) transition, and (5) improvement. The priori-

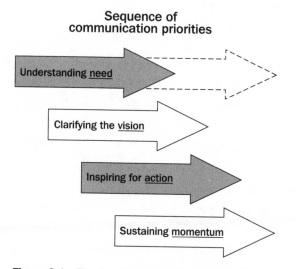

Figure 8.1 The four communication priorities.

ties break down as follows: (1) explaining the need for action, (2) clarifying the vision, (3) inspiring for action, and (4) sustaining momentum.

Let's consider each in turn, and discuss the communication vehicles that best support each priority.

Action Tips

TIP▶ Explain the Need for Action

In any action, people's first and last question will be some version of *why*.

From start to finish, you will have to address such questions as the following:

Why do we need this?

What's wrong with the way we are doing things now?

What will the action do for employees?

What happens if we are not successful?

Does this mean fewer jobs?

Is this something to worry about or look forward to?

The *why* question is not always easy to answer, particularly if the company is profitable and there are no apparent problems. You have to convince people that you are preparing for the future, not attempting to remedy the past.

In addressing this first priority, how you choose to launch your action program is a critical decision. The choice tends to be driven mostly by your action path.

In most cases, the longer-duration decathlons and marathons are best launched in a low-key way. Because of the often lengthy time between the start of actions and the point at which actions actually pay off, it is better not to raise interest and expectations too high if no immediate steps are required.

Conversely, the shorter-running sprints and high jumps are likely to demand either a higher-profile launch or a means of getting information out to people quickly.

The following three high-impact communication vehicles can be used to explain the case for action and to launch actions of varying length.

1. Briefing Cascade

This communication process harnesses what we call the *boss principle*, taking advantage of the unique relationship that exists between employees and their bosses at all levels. Here's how it works:

Senior managers brief middle managers, who, in turn, brief frontline employees. As John Eaton, managing director of Barclaycard, says, "The best way to get the communication process really working is to get line managers and supervisors developing a sense of ownership for *wanting* to get the message through the business."

A sample cascade agenda might include a recap of vision and values, possibly using a video featuring the chief executive officer; the case for action; actions to move the organization forward; your role in the action; and feedback on the briefing.

Remember that most employees expect and wish to hear important information directly from their supervisors. And these managers are uniquely placed to be able to interpret the information for those employees.

On the flip side, a supervisor who is not fully engaged in the action process is the one person whose behavior can stymie the progress made by communicating through other channels.

2. Mobilization Workshops

In longer actions, a powerful vehicle for explaining the need is to combine the cascade approach with a workshop format. The sessions are attended by subsequent tiers of employees—managers first, then frontline people—in groups of 10 to 50.

The trick is to give each group time to internalize the action specifics—both during and after the workshop—before asking it to lead workshops with the next tier.

One drawback is that workshops are very resource-intensive, and they usually cannot cover the entire organization. They also demand substantial involvement by the leader and top team to demonstrate their commitment.

On the plus side, though, this communication vehicle demands instant participation. It also allows time to respond to objections, and it pushes people to commit to the activity.

3. E-mail or Memo from the Action Leader
It may seem obvious, but it works.

In actions that are better suited to a low profile or that require an immediate introductory communication, a simple e-mail or paper memo to all staff members can explain what the action is about and lay out an elementary case for the action.

E-mail has the advantage of providing wide coverage for a consistent message. It also allows the sender to, in effect, play down the action while laying the groundwork for more communication later.

There are some disadvantages, though. E-mail depersonalizes the communication. It is one-way. It can carry only a few lines (that is, if you expect anybody to read it).

Also, e-mail from the action manager conflicts with the boss principle, so it might be seen as less trustworthy and credible.

▶
LEARN BY EXAMPLE: **Shell Information Services**

Here's one page of the communication that action leaders at Shell Information Services frequently used to answer the *why* question:

> Both SCIS and IS have built up their own services and reputation. However, we live in a very competitive world. There are lots of service providers eager to take our business. Having two IT organiza-

tions reduces our competitiveness. By eliminating overlaps and releasing synergies, we can improve existing services and increase our capability to develop new ones. We need clearer access, integrated account management, and simplified commercial arrangements for our customers' benefit.

Together we can add more value to the Group. By exploiting our joint capabilities, we can better contribute to delivery of the businesses' strategies in all their areas of operation. We can offer staff a greater professional and career challenge in an integrated IT organization. We need a single brand with a strong image.

◄

TIP► Keep Explaining the Need for Action

Here are our suggestions:

Concentrate initially on explaining why the action is being taken rather than what the action is.

Complete these sentences in 10 or fewer words: "We need to take action because . . ." "You need to take action because . . ."

Make the action leader the initial voice of any launch communication, but maximize the boss principle in providing follow-up clarity, context, and commitment.

Review the opportunity to use either cascade briefings, mobilization workshops, or action e-mails to launch the action with the correct profile.

Reinforce the message with supporting media, including dedicated newsletters, corporate news media, and agenda items at regular briefing events.

Build a question-and-answer package that provides good, consistent answers to the *why* questions posed by stakeholders.

Be cautious about criticizing the past, always remembering that your audience is part of the history that you are denouncing.

Use a feedback questionnaire within each primary vehicle to assess people's understanding and belief in the case for action, the potential benefits, the key stages, and the duration of the action program.

TIP▶ Clarify Your Action's Vision

If one sees best and farthest at the top of the mountain, then only the few who climb that high can enjoy the vista unimpeded. Most everyone else remains in the valley, awaiting word on what the territory looks like from an otherwise inaccessible vantage point.

Certainly, not all of these people need to see the landscape in its broadest expanse. Perhaps most don't even want to see it, for that matter.

But if those few hardy souls who scale the heights expect the continued respect and support of their fellows, then they'd best be prepared to explain what it is that they see so clearly.

The key questions you must address as you begin communication to clarify the vision for your action include the following:

What exactly is the vision? Why this vision and not another?

How does this action fit with our strategy and with other initiatives going on?

How will our work be different?

Will this mean new procedures or revised reporting lines?

Will this action give us more or less authority?

Is this just for the troops or do managers need to change as well?

Will we be consulted in the design process?

The specifics of the vision usually begin to take shape in the earliest stages of a business action. The first step might be something as simple as a summary of the key elements of the action and how they fit together.

Going forward, the communication process can be both the means for testing ideas with people as the vision evolves and the vehicle for disseminating the final packaged form.

As our work with global companies illustrates, a vision can be communicated using anything from a single diagram to a comprehensive design of how the new organization will look and operate.

High-impact vehicles for clarifying the vision include the following:

1. Vision Presentations
These are usually conducted with groups of 10 to 20 employees at a time once the vision is finalized. Both a line manager and a member of the action team who can answer more technical questions will probably preside.

Presentations require piloting and some degree of customization for the local audience. They should be supported with strong visuals and takeaway materials for further reading.

This vehicle is a great way for the boss to demonstrate both a grasp of the action and a commitment to it.

2. One-on-One Meetings
Regular meetings to discuss the emerging vision are a good way to involve and communicate with key people such as managers and influential frontline employees.

Such meetings build commitment before the message is presented to the wider organization. But they are resource-intensive, so you need to be selective about where you direct the effort.

▶

───

LEARN BY EXAMPLE: **Barclaycard**

It is the market leader among credit card operations in the United Kingdom, but Barclaycard knows that it cannot afford to stay closed up at home in hopes that the neighborhood won't change. Vision communication, in various guises, is very much a part of its effort.

To emphasize the interdependence among key parts of the organization's vision, Barclaycard managers came up with a simple drawing, shown in Figure 8.2, of five pillars holding up the roof of a house.

Executive sponsor Peter Herbert, then finance director and one of the executives who championed the idea at an early stage, notes, somewhat quizzically, that the depiction looks more like a Greek temple. But the idea is to convey to employees the message that the company's promise to its customers—its value proposition—is supported by the five initiatives and the employees who bring them to reality.

The company designed posters and communication packages using the house metaphor to persuade employees that they are all in this action together. Anyone who falters in his or her role threatens the whole.

Or, as Herbert puts it, "Each plays a part in holding up the whole structure. You can't have just one or two on their own, or the promise falls to ruins."

The House of Pillars also became the theme for Barclaycard's mobi-

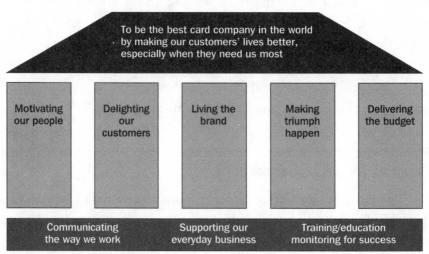

Figure 8.2 Barclaycard's vision.

lization workshops. Executives introduced each pillared initiative and role-plays were used to illustrate them.

───◄

TIP► Keep Clarifying the Vision

Here's how we suggest you go about it:

Devise one simple graphic that clearly states the key elements of the vision.

Turn the vision inside out. Ask: What does it mean for each stakeholder? What are the threats? What are the benefits?

Look for opportunities to build communication into core action-program activities like meetings and workshops, rather than creating too many dedicated communication events.

Use a feedback questionnaire in conjunction with each high-impact vehicle to gauge people's understanding and belief in the key vision elements. You also want to assess how they perceive the main implications for themselves individually.

TIP► Inspire for Action

As implementation approaches, employees need the kinds of details that will inspire their commitment.

Besides expecting more details (and rightly so), they inevitably are concerned with the personal implications of the action.

Some of the questions you must be prepared to answer include the following:

How will my job be different?

Will this affect my career prospects and terms and conditions?

When will I know exactly what this means for my job role?

What training will I receive?

When will the new environment actually begin?

Who is responsible for leading the action in my area?

One communications priority is to inspire people to take on the challenges delineated by the action team, to build their work lives around those imperatives, and to move quickly to implement them.

This priority applies to all four of our action paths, but if you are conducting a sprint or a high jump, it will probably top your list. Both sprinters and high jumpers have to act quickly to reach their desired performance levels.

A word to decathlon participants and marathon runners: You still need to pay close attention to this part of the sequence, although with less urgency.

When the *me* questions grow more insistent, communication needs to take place in smaller groups to ensure an effective and more personalized message.

The boss principle moves to center stage. One-on-one or team meetings, rather than larger-scale methods such as video presentations, also become increasingly important.

We suggest three high-impact vehicles to inspire for action:

1. One-on-One Briefings
These critical meetings between the boss and individual team members have a two-part agenda: a presentation of what the action means for the individual, followed by a discussion of the issues and concerns that arise.

2. Action News Flash via E-mail or Posted on an Intranet
As implementation approaches, a good deal of operational information often needs to be communicated in increasingly frequent bursts. E-mail is an excellent vehicle.

3. Action Orientation or Training

The orientation or training events in this phase should give more details about the action than were provided in the earlier vision presentations. In some cases, education and skills development are central to the agenda.

As such, the approach is more participatory. People explore the new working approaches through customized simulations, role-playing, or case studies.

The communication opportunity often comes at the front or back of the agenda, where the line manager can take an active role.

▶ ───

LEARN BY EXAMPLE: British Airways Engineering

British Airways' decision to embark on an ambitious three-year program to reengineer its maintenance operations so as to make them world class put it on a decathlon action path. And the enormity of the action moved the communication process to the forefront to explain what the vision meant for individuals.

There's sometimes a hidden agenda when communicating action, reflects managing director Brian Philpott:

> One of the things I learned was that people meant two things when they asked me to explain the strategy.
>
> I'd stand up there and talk to people, or even sit across the table with individuals, and people would say, "What's the strategy?" I'd reply with something along the lines of, "You've got the strategy. Everybody has the strategy. I presented it at the staff day."
>
> What they were really saying, of course—but were too scared to articulate—is what does the strategy actually do to me? Once I realized that you have to answer two questions—not only explain the

strategy but also what it means for individuals—then it became a lot easier.

Plus, that way, you get a contract of engagement with every person in the business, which is invaluable.

With implementation some months away, BA decided to introduce the vision in presentations to small groups.

It created a cartoon, shown on a giant screen, that was designed to present the vision of the "new world": how aircraft would now be maintained and how the supporting chain of activities that involved every BA Engineering employee would operate. People could see just what the new world was about and how it would be different.

More than a thousand people attended the presentations. Copies of the cartoon were also made available for road shows in remote locations.

As the first wave of implementation approached, BA Engineering intensified communication with a three-stage orientation program. Project manager Ray Claydon relates how the stages worked:

> Stage 1, which was hosted by the managing director, tried to explain how we would look and function over the next few years. We used a professional interviewer to field questions from the audience.
>
> In Stage 2, we had a lot more fun, with an agenda set up to communicate how we would work in our new teams. The activities included a timed pit stop on a Formula 1 racing car with everyone working with their new teams against the clock. People still remember it! We allowed plenty of breaks for questions and answers, and included presentations from fleet general managers.

One of the fleet managers, Keith Mitchell, takes up the story:

> Stage 3, which was positioned following our first "go live" dates, was more challenging for us. Our focus was on the individual and

building the tools and skills needed to perform jobs based on training needs.

Day-to-day operational pressures made it much harder to cover
all the required people.

The first wave of implementation was completed on schedule. And
even though embedding the moves took longer than expected, BA
Engineering is now seeing significant improvements in performance.

TIP▶ Keep Inspiring Employees to Action

Here is our list of specific suggestions to keep you on track:

Ensure that the key message about what the action means for each
individual is delivered by the employee's manager or team leader.

Review the potential for using one-on-one briefings, orientation programs, and e-mail news flashes.

Start coaching managers early on their behavior and ability to counsel; the most powerful communication starts when the formal communication events stop.

Use a feedback questionnaire in conjunction with each high-impact
vehicle to assess people's understanding of the actions as they apply
to them. You also want to gauge their knowledge of how and when
moves will be made and how and when training will be provided.

TIP▶ Communicate to Sustain Momentum

You are entering the final stage of the action program. Nothing sends
a clearer message that the job is completed than a declaration that the
company is about to "go live" with the action.

But there's a problem: Real improvements may be months away.
Action must be ongoing, and fine-tuning will be needed after the program is up and running.

So the challenge for the action communicator, then, is to sustain a high profile.

Answering the following questions is part of maintaining that profile:

How will we be kept informed as we approach the "go-live" date?

What support will we receive after training?

Are we actually achieving any improvements?

Will there be any recognition for successful action?

To sustain momentum, consider using the following three high-impact vehicles. All are useful throughout the transition, but they are particularly effective in sustaining momentum.

1. Progress Newsletters

These may be deployed at any time in the action process, but they are particularly powerful for providing clear summaries of progress to dispersed groups of employees later in the initiative.

A progress newsletter should report performance improvements, showcase employees who are thriving on the action, and profile quick wins.

2. Intranet Updates

Self-contained corporate computer networks can be used to showcase the work of teams, individuals, departments, or action programs.

An intranet is particularly useful after the resource-intensive action infrastructure has been scaled back and a more efficient means of reaching employees is called for. Intranets are increasingly being used to keep people up to date on demand.

3. Communicate through Leadership Action

Surprised to see this technique included in a discussion about communication?

You won't be after we tell you that 70 percent of *real* communication comes from doing and only 30 percent comes from vocalizing about it.

As an action manager, you may well find yourself coaching your action leader on ways to communicate desired modifications and behavior via role modeling. (Turn back to Chapter 5 to review the specific suggestions we make for helping your leader to role model.)

▶ ──

Learn by Example: Adaptec, Inc.

To better understand how a company can successfully use communications to sustain momentum, consider Adaptec. Here is a company that set out to redesign its processes, install SAP technology to improve manufacturing, order fulfillment, materials procurement, and customer service—*and* become a $1-billion business, all in less than 2 years.

Headquartered in Silicon Valley, Adaptec employs about 1,500 people to conduct research, develop new products, handle order fulfillment, and manage operations. Another 800 employees work at its production center in Singapore. Adaptec had attempted two earlier action projects, both of which failed after only a few months.

As might be expected for a leader in the high-tech industry, Adaptec already had an internal communications system in place, specifically one supporting an intranet with e-mail capability.

Unfortunately, when the company first announced its action project in 1996, that system did not extend all the way to Singapore, although the company has since spanned the Pacific electronically.

Nevertheless, here was an ideal medium to directly communicate with large numbers of people at the speed demanded by a sprint, and to invite their feedback on proposals to streamline operations, cut costs, and improve customer service.

What's more, the intranet allowed access to the SAP Web site in Germany, through which employees could receive information about systems and process improvements.

Employees could see for themselves that mere incremental improvements in quality were insufficient to help the company reach its goals. The quantum leaps in research, development, and performance promised by the action project were what was needed to maintain and increase market share.

Evidencing the popularity of Adaptec's intranet, the action program site registered up to 4,000 internal visitors in 1 month, roughly 3 visits for each employee in the United States. Not all employees had access to the company's intranet, though, so project manager Jim Schmidt also used traditional paper-based media to get the message out.

Communications manager Ed Moore developed a newsletter, appropriately entitled *Changing Times,* for distribution to all stakeholders. The newsletter also became a regular feature on the intranet page.

Schmidt and Moore recognized—and you should, too—that the printed page is still a valuable tool, especially when enhanced with photographs, graphics, and frequent quotations.

Adaptec did not rely only on the intranet and newsletters to sustain momentum. Managers presented the action project at every quarterly employee meeting.

The messages initially reached audiences totaling some 700 employees. The reach was expanded when tapes were sent out to employees in remote locations.

In addition, project managers often talked with small groups of employees over lunch, or met with focus groups to check their understanding of the need for action.

Gina Gloski, director of manufacturing, found these meetings to be among the most beneficial of Adaptec's communications, particularly because they reached people who worked late shifts or irregular hours. Gloski says this group is oftentimes excluded from the daily flow of memos and information.

◀

Tip▶ Keep Sustaining Momentum

Here are our suggestions:

Beware the trap of believing that repetition is duplication. It isn't. Careful repetition reinforces a message.

Publicize a major "win" at least every three to six months.

Use a feedback questionnaire in conjunction with each high-impact vehicle to assess people's commitment to the action. You also want to know how they see the improvements in their own areas.

Action Paths

Here's our advice on developing good communications programs for each action path.

▶Action Path Sprint

The message: "We must catch up; we are behind." This is best communicated with "shock-wave" presentations that starkly represent the gravity of the situation and lay out the first, urgent moves.

Continuously update progress—performance versus the target goal; break it down locally so everyone knows the weak links. Include contributions from everyone—from the chief executive to frontline employees.

Use e-mail for instantaneous, universal progress reporting. Reiterate urgency.

▶ACTION PATH   High Jump

Make communicating the action imperative the first challenge—why the move, why so fast?

Use frequent e-mail and face-to-face communication; the system has to be faster than the rumor machine. Display a countdown graphic in prominent locations.

Use numerous media repetitively; people rarely take in a message the first time, especially when things are moving quickly.

▶ACTION PATH   Decathlon

The message: "We have to run just to stand still; we have to run *like hell* if we want to get ahead." Use hard facts from market intelligence and customer feedback to overcome complacency and raise the urgency level.

Use evidence from other locations to prove that the action is working.

Make education part of the mix—take people to witness best practices or bring best practices to them.

Communicate to international locations through a careful balance of local and company language.

Reduce the action's vision to a single icon that can be understood globally.

▶ACTION PATH   Marathon

Use periodic bursts of communication to raise the action profile and sustain interest; spot bonuses that reward desired performance are an effective way to do this.

Design icons that capture the key elements of the action and use them throughout the organization.

Have leaders and managers take symbolic actions that reinforce their commitment; if necessary, run a workshop with senior executives to select these actions.

Get senior leadership out on the front lines talking about the importance of the action.

Celebrate intermediate successes.

Have periodic spirit-raising events.

Organize road shows to take the message out to all corners of the organization.

Questions and Answers

QUESTION: How important is the communication component of an action?

Absolutely crucial. There are four primary reasons why communication is so essential:

1. It enlists stakeholder support by providing compelling reasons for the action.

2. By responding honestly to questions, it clarifies the vision and increases buy-in.

3. It informs and inspires people, making them partners in the action.

4. Through regular updates, it sustains momentum and keeps the action on course, even over the long haul.

QUESTION: My company has a central communications function. Will it be sufficient for the action?

Probably not. Many respondents found their existing communications infrastructure to be inadequate to support the demands of a large action program. Additional channels were required, resources had to be put into place at locations outside headquarters, and the communications skills of line managers had to be sharpened.

Existing channels are rarely sufficient for several reasons. For one thing, an action program places a greater emphasis on face-to-face communication. In addition, the focus shifts from communicating information to changing attitudes and behaviors. Third, action communication must be almost instantaneously responsive to feedback from stakeholder groups.

Finally, since action programs have a significant impact on individuals, the grapevine will work overtime to fill any communication vacuum—and this ancient mode of dissemination is rife with distortion, embellishment, and selective hearing. Thus, new communication channels—such as electronic rumor boards, where employees can anonymously post rumors and managers can nip distortions in the bud—are required to ensure that the grapevine is made obsolete.

QUESTION: Does action communication differ from region to region?

Yes. The differences between Eastern and Western approaches are vivid. At several Asian companies, for example, we noted that employee newsletters were almost brutally frank, that employees were encouraged to openly question their managers about the veracity of communications, and that board meetings were televised. In marked contrast, managers in Western countries were unwilling to communicate poor performance reports and feared having to face the troops. They often disclosed the tough messages only at the last possible moment.

Time after time—no matter where their location—our respondents mentioned the importance of trustworthy communications. An Australian action manager wisely observes: "The truth will eventually come out, and once you've been caught lying, it's very hard, perhaps impossible, to regain people's trust."

Beyond the often humorous, sometimes embarrassing mistakes that are made when messages from headquarters are translated into local languages, the sheer diversity of employees dictates regional nuances in wording. Cultural peculiarities, too, make a standardized approach unworkable.

In Singapore, where cultural conformity simplifies communications, a survey respondent said, "We tell people what we want them to do when we are clear and ready, and employees are then expected to proceed." In Germany and elsewhere, work councils (union bodies) often review and approve of all communications that go to employees. In Japan, face-to-face communication is preferred, while more and more companies in the United States are making use of intranets to support communication activity.

The implication for the global action manager, then, is clear: Establish a local communications infrastructure to test, customize, deliver, and feed back information.

QUESTION: Our chief executive (and action leader) wants to launch our action program. I think we should use line managers. Who's right?

Your CEO. Our case studies have shown that the action leader, not the line manager, is the best person to oversee the launch. The baton is then passed to the line managers, who can provide local clarity and build buy-in.

At a number of companies we surveyed, action programs were launched with a statement of the new corporate vision and values—often before the ink had dried on the design of the program. Few things seem more irrelevant and platitudinous to an employee than a high-minded statement delivered without substantial supporting actions and a clear explanation of its personal implications. The action manager must resist executive pressure to launch before a detailed program of follow-through is in place.

QUESTION: How can I measure the efficacy of my action communication?

It's crucial for the action manager to measure the quality of communication throughout the life of the program. Rapid feedback is important, and many conventional measurement tools may be too time-consuming. As a simple litmus test of how well you are getting the message across, why not use a set of questions that can be asked of groups or individuals in workshops or meetings, or even at home on their own time. Anonymity may increase the level of honesty.

Be sure to record responses to the questions verbatim. They are invaluable for revising the communications agenda and giving feedback to the action leadership. They will probably be shocked by what the employees say—and they may well be motivated to put more effort and care into communication.

QUESTION: My background is in sales and I believe action communications can learn a lot from basic sales principles. Do you agree?

Absolutely. We've interviewed a number of action managers who find it helpful to think of communications in terms of a marketing program. Your "consumers," of course, are the organization's employees and stakeholders. Once you make this assumption, certain helpful truths and tools become evident:

1. There is no God-given dictum saying that consumers *have* to buy your "product." Consumers will buy (and continue to buy) only if they are genuinely convinced that they have a need. Job survival is a powerful need.

2. Have the facts to back up your claims. Use both quantitative and qualitative research; the former is needed to build a solid case, and the latter can help in framing communications.

3. Manage expectations by setting realistic plans and milestones, phased in over time, and ensure that you communicate these clearly to all concerned, both at the start and during the process.

4. Be aware of the competition. What parallel initiatives might distract from yours? Put together an integrated plan that takes competitive events into account.

5. Focus your messages by limiting each communication to a single central point, bolstered with supporting evidence. This is the principle behind effective advertising, and it works. We're all suffering from information overload these days; you have to cut through the verbiage.

6. Repetition, repetition, repetition. Don't assume that once you have communicated, that's it. Use multiple media—coming from all directions—with each one reinforcing the others.

7. Customize your message to address the needs of each consumer segment.

8. Focus on benefits. What's in it for the audience? Keep asking *so what?* until you have defined the real benefit.

9. Appeal to both the rational and the emotional. People react both ways. Don't be afraid to appeal to emotions—they're powerful drivers of human response.

10. Anticipate objections and resistance from the start. Work out how to counter it and prepare your "salespeople" for effective dialogue with "customers."

11. Treat your action champions as a sales force. Support their selling efforts; offer sales conferences, presentation materials, and sales training.

12. Use branding to bring the program to life. Give your program a name, develop a design style and logo, and use it on everything that you publish, disseminate, or produce.

13. Be aware of the product life cycle. Your initiative will go through a growth and decline curve, just like every new product. Know where you are on the curve—and refresh your program with a jolt of new energy *before* your consumers grow tired.

9

THE SEVENTH CHALLENGE— CULTIVATE FOR ACTION

We don't call it human resources for nothing. People are a resource—rich, sacred, varied, volatile, and finite: They can be depleted. But if cultivated with skill and care, they can be tapped nearly to their limit, and then renewed.

Managing action is like skippering a ship through a storm. While your hands are on the wheel and your eyes are on your charts, who is taking care of the crew?

On your company's ship, the answer is *human resources.*

Traditionally, human resources has dealt with recruitment, compensation, and benefits—the standard people issues of every organization. It has been the traffic cop, the gatekeeper for entering and exiting employees, and the enforcer of internal personnel policies.

But business has changed. Action has become a way of life. The employee life cycle consists of a series of journeys, each of which encounters the key dimensions of people policy.

And human resources must move with the times. It must be drawn from its supporting role into the heart of the action.

There, a whole new identity awaits. And you, as an action manager, will need to identify and coordinate human-resource policies to support your action needs. This chapter will show you how.

To make the most of what human resources has to offer, from beginning to end of your action, pay heed to the four areas of people policy that are the core of people management:

1. Recruitment and selection

2. Training and development

3. Recognition and compensation

4. Migration and transition

We believe that these four categories encompass the definitive policies and processes, those that touch every single employee at some point on his or her journey through your organization. Here is where people policies can make a difference to your action's progress.

People policies traditionally facilitate continuity and stability. Actions, by their very nature, tend to clash with that conservative approach: They exist to *modify* behaviors and results, not to continue them.

This means that you will have the opportunity—indeed, the obligation—to establish brand-new people policies for your action.

What? you gasp. *Revamp procedures? Rewrite guidelines?* Relax. Wholesale revamping of the human-resources policies and department is not what's wanted.

Your number-one concern is getting your action off the ground. So you will largely be looking at policies that affect your project team. Still, the team can become, in effect, the microcosm for more far-reaching shifts in people policy.

Draw on team members' responses to guide you as you roll out the action to the parts of the wider organization that are most directly affected by it. Of course, not all of the people policies you've implemented for the team will travel well.

That's okay. What matters is the muscle-building you've done. You've broadened your knowledge and increased your skills. That can only help when you find yourself addressing people policies for a wider audience.

As the world of action expands and expands, your policies quite probably will have even more far-reaching influence, particularly if you've enlisted the support of human-resources personnel for your action project.

In that event, your model may very likely provide the template for the whole organization's people policies down the road.

But for now, let's look at each of the main human-resources issues in turn.

Action Tips

TIP▶ Tap the Experience of Your Human-Resources People to Build Your Action Team

Action means movement, and accelerated movement at that. The immediate question at hand is: How will you find the right 20, or 40, or 100 people to populate your action team—today?

A human-resources department with the capabilities to formally assess potential action-team candidates can play a pivotal role in the selection process.

By taking advantage of these capabilities, you can more easily identify team members who bring the mix of knowledge, skills, and attributes you are seeking. That mix might include, among other things, knowledge of strategies, operations, systems, and processes, as well as team-building and reengineering techniques.

Analytical skills and creativity might also be deemed important, along with a bent for risk taking and dealing with ambiguity. Executive stakeholders can also be key advisors in identifying and securing the right people for your action team.

But no matter what you are looking for, the advantage lies in being able to rely on the expertise of experienced professionals to help you find who and what you need more quickly and effectively.

Good human-resource function capabilities can make it easier to understand what measures are acceptable to use in extracting people from their current positions. Some companies are willing to backfill behind people who leave to join the action team; others insist that the work left behind be picked up by those still managing the day-to-day operations.

When human-resources managers understand the strategic management of human assets—maintaining succession-planning and knowledge-and-skills databases, for example—you can use those capabilities to move forward rapidly, grooming high-potential people and strengthening the team-recruitment process.

Bringing together the right mix of aptitudes and attitudes is obviously a tall order, even when you have the support of human resources. You want to target the best and the brightest to join the action team. To make sure that you don't overlook potential winners, cast your net far and wide.

▶─────────────────────────────

LEARN BY EXAMPLE: **The Neiman Marcus Group, Inc.**

At Neiman Marcus, strong human-resources capabilities paid big dividends when Chief Operating Officer Gerald Sampson proposed a major reengineering of the specialty retailer's processes.

Human-resources executive Manuel Zaby was heavily involved in the action program from the outset, and he is credited with putting together a highly motivated, cross-functional project team that included sales associates and department heads as well as key executives.

Thanks to Zaby's foresight, Neiman Marcus had frontline employees at the table whose practical experience was critical to uncovering the barriers the action plan had to overcome.

LEARN BY EXAMPLE: Bristol-Myers Squibb

With 30-plus manufacturing plants and 20,000 to 25,000 employees affected in 20 countries, Bristol-Myers Squibb was pushing for a championship performance when it undertook its massive demand-management action project.

Knowing that meeting each successive challenge in this decathlon posed a formidable task, the company wisely included a couple of practice hurdle runs in the form of two pilot projects—one in Ireland, the other in the United States.

These pilots were carefully chosen: The company wanted them to be big enough to be credible but not so big as to be overly complex. And, needless to say, they needed to be successful.

Mindful of the project's global nature, the company initially recruited team members from all seven of its divisions and from every region in which it operates. The team members were on loan and remained on the payrolls of their respective parent plants, which, as project manager Dana Cooper so vividly explains, ensured that the sites "continued to have skin in the game."

In other words, the sending sites maintained a vested interest in the project design by virtue of their personal connection to specific team members. The team members, in turn, were continually managing stakeholders by keeping their bosses back home up to date on the project's progress.

The global, cross-functional nature of the team-selection process also headed off another unwanted side effect: It made it impossible for the far-flung pieces of the company to shrug off the project as only a U.S. initiative, or, for that matter, as only for pharmaceuticals, or consumer goods, or medical devices.

◄

TIP▶ Know What to Train For

Every athlete knows the importance of training. So does every business leader. The question for the action manager, then, is not whether to train, but how to pull off the right kind of training in a compressed time frame.

First, make sure that your team and individual training derives from a valid assessment of the technical, process, and general business skills and knowledge needed to pull off the action. Coupling an awareness of those needs with an assessment of each individual's abilities allows you to put in place specific training and development plans for each team member.

The ultimate goal of knowledge and skills assessment is to arrive at an overall knowledge-acquisition plan. The plan lays out the exact training each individual team member will be receiving at specific times and at particular locations.

Mapping out individual needs determines training priorities and helps to ensure that knowledge and skills acquisition will occur in a timely manner at strategic locations. In other words, you are making sure that your project team members have the right knowledge and skills at the right time to get their jobs done.

From the team members' perspective, the assessment process demonstrates that their growth and development is being accelerated and that they will acquire specific new skills, skills that probably will make them more competitive for positions both internally and externally.

This added benefit can motivate their involvement and performance during the action.

To plan for effective knowledge acquisition, ask yourself these questions:

What skills and knowledge can each individual contribute to the action?

What skills and/or knowledge are required to do a job effectively; how will these vary over the duration of the action?

What skills- and knowledge-development goals exist for each action-team member?

Where do the skills and knowledge that each individual needs to perform his or her work and to reach personal development goals reside? (Think of veteran employees, classroom training, relevant databases, and so forth, within the project and in and out of the organization.)

What media and other vehicles will be used to transfer that knowledge?

Tip▶ Get Support Facilities in Place

It almost goes without saying that having the appropriate technical and nontechnical support facilities in place and readily available to all team members is one of the keys to successful training and development.

These include not only facilities for discrete, formal training sessions, but also facilities that enable more informal knowledge and skills development—for example, "war rooms" where project information and issues can be clearly displayed on the walls, and where space is available for impromptu meetings between team members.

Another successful training strategy is to co-locate action-project members with one another so as to enable the strategic transfer of resident knowledge and skills.

▶

LEARN BY EXAMPLE: **The Neiman Marcus Group, Inc.**

The Neiman Marcus process-reengineering program was supported by weekly education and development materials sent to managers and staff. Issues ran the gamut from new customer-loyalty programs, to point-of-sale computer-terminal capabilities that enable optimum selling, to stress-management techniques.

Each week, the education and development staff sent out a new package to department managers alerting them to the week's topic, telling them exactly what material to cover, how to spark discussion, and which questions to ask on any given day. The managers then spent anywhere from 15 minutes to a maximum of 30 minutes a day in mini–training sessions with their staffs.

◀

TIP▶ Offer Attractive Incentives

Whether you want to admit it, or not, successfully bringing your action program to fruition is, at some point, unequivocally connected with recognition and compensation.

Put another way, compensation is not the one thing that will make everything go all right, but it could be the one thing that gets in the way of everything going right.

Research done by Exxon Corporation found that while mission statements posted in an office induced desired behavior in only 2 percent of the staff, the number shot up to 55 percent virtually overnight when rewards were aligned with the action.

Beyond confirming what psychologists have long known—that positive reinforcement is a powerful incentive—another hard truth makes it imperative that you come up with a viable plan for rewarding and compensating your team: To entice and hold onto the caliber of people you need to effectively implement and sustain your action program, you may have to offer very attractive incentives.

The sticking point may be in determining which incentives to offer.

Without question, you must align your system of rewards with the direction and milestones of your action program as well as with the company's strategic business plan. Besides the positive boost the program receives when people are rewarded for furthering its goals, fairness demands that those who come onto the project team are sufficiently rewarded.

▶ ─────────────────────────────────────

Learn by Example: Adaptec, Inc.

As Paul Hansen, chief financial officer at Adaptec, aptly observes, "People stepping out of their normal career paths for two years and engaging themselves in a large-scale action project fear that they will lose out careerwise." (You will recall that Adaptec chose to sprint to the finish line in its companywide program to overhaul processes and systems.)

To make sure that Adaptec project members didn't pay a price, the company engaged its human-resources people to design an appropriate reward system that provided for attractive stock and bonus incentives.

Learn by Example: Bank Corporation

The situation was similar at Bank Corporation, where the finance operation decided to boost performance.

Recognizing that big moves are hard, and cognizant of the fact that more than $45 million in annual savings was at stake in its plan to centralize its entire finance operation, the bank put its money behind a claim that it *paid for performance.*

Thus, bonuses for senior finance people were tied to the success of the action plan: If the shareholders won, so would the people who made it happen. Depending on the level of the person involved, bonuses ranged from 25 percent up to 100 percent—all funded from money saved by the action program.

◄

TIP► Find the Right Fit

What is right for one company may not be right for another. That's because incentives must at once fit into a corporate culture and be of motivating value to different employees with disparate attitudes about what constitutes a reward. The wrong reward may be worse than no reward at all. For example, although lunch with the chief executive officer might be exhilarating for a marketing manager, a line worker or someone in research and development might consider it more a trial than a treat.

By the same token, financial incentives that are too low can spark cynicism and negativism among employees if they perceive the reward potential as a joke or a slap in the face.

To be effective as a motivational tool, we have found that cash rewards must equal at least 5 to 8 percent of salary. (This is on top of any other bonus program for which an employee is eligible.) Noncash awards must equal about 4 percent of salary to bring about a shift in behavior.

One noncash reward that has proved successful for several companies with which we work is a three-day weekend at a local resort.

The hotel is paid for and a room credit is established so the recipient can take advantage of the facility. The extra day off is part of the award. That way, the employee doesn't have to use a vacation day.

Simple, lower-cost programs that encourage frequent recognition of behavior and results can be quite effective, too. One company has instituted a peer recognition program in which employees recognize each other on the spot with "project dollars." The scrip can be spent at periodic auctions of company merchandise.

A word of caution about rewards: Highly rewarding a select few for stepping outside the normal boundaries can easily breed resentment among those who continue to get out the daily product. Not everyone will readily understand the career risks being taken by the action participants, and the tension can become palpable.

TIP▶ Involve Employees in Designing Incentives

You may be surprised to discover that money is not always the reward of choice.

On one project, teams were asked to take a week to think through and then answer, in writing, the following question: "What incentives would make this the absolute best project with which you've ever been involved, one you would be willing to see through until its completion?"

Initially, the answer that rang out was, "Money!" Yet, after a week of thought, teams returned with a variety of unexpected incentive structures. Many did not include money as a reward.

TIP▶ Allow Participants to Choose from a Menu of Rewards

Giving individuals some choice—say, from among merchandise prizes, stock, cash, travel vouchers, status, self-development, privileges, or leisure time—has a greater capacity to motivate a wider group of participants. It also ensures that behavior is focused on earning rewards that have the most meaning while still achieving the intended action results.

TIP▶ Establish Team Rewards and Let Teams Identify Meaningful Incentives

Both teamwork and team rewards are empowering, and team accomplishments are easier and more effective to measure than is individual effort. Moreover, when a team jointly shares a difficult reward, team bonds are strengthened and the win becomes part of team and company history.

Pay careful attention, however, to whether team members, leaders, sponsors, and project managers are rewarded the same or differently. Decide how rewards will be arranged and distributed—tangible and intangible, work and nonwork, management and nonmanagement, team and individual, and so forth.

T<small>IP</small>▶ Tie Team-Based Compensation to Predetermined Goals for Business, Team, and Individual Performance

Defining expected results, criteria, and measures clarifies the correctness of the system and engenders the enthusiasm of those who will participate. Criteria establish standards of performance for determining awards and provide guidelines for tracking and fine-tuning incentives and rewards over time.

Good criteria are simple, specific, attainable, and few in number. The idea is to set up ways that help people succeed, not cause them to fail. Simply decide what will be measured and how often.

▶────────────────────────────────────

LEARN BY EXAMPLE: **Bank Corporation**

Julia Kuhl, senior vice president of finance at Bank Corporation, considers both results and behaviors when making end-of-year bonus recommendations. And she makes certain that everyone knows what's expected:

> More than once, I have emphasized what these behaviors are so that people know that I expect teamwork, responsiveness, responsibility—meaning don't drop the ball—and communication with each other.

LEARN BY EXAMPLE: SkyChefs, Inc.

At SkyChefs, everyone—from the presidents at the top of the organization, down through the area vice presidents and operating executives in the service groups, to the steering teams in the various geographic areas—is compensated based on models that look at personal behavior and the achievement of organizational goals.

At the team level, the functional units are judged on how effectively they deploy assets and resources to meet business needs overall, whereas individuals are scored both on their performance of specific functional duties—say, improving operations in Madrid—as well as on their contribution to the broader goals in Europe.

TIP▶ Certify People in the Skills Required for a New Job, Then Link Completion of Certified Training Modules to Remuneration

The first step in certification is to standardize processes, and that, in turn, will allow you to standardize jobs throughout the organization.

LEARN BY EXAMPLE: Bristol-Myers Squibb

This is what Bristol-Myers Squibb is attempting to do as its massive project unfolds.

Once grading levels and requisite job skills are equivalent from site to site, says Project Director Dana Cooper, you can institute a certification process based on a specific set of knowledge and skill expectations.

As Cooper envisions it, certification will not only maintain standards, but also will make employees eligible for advancement opportunities.

Whatever reward and incentive system you come up with, make sure that top management supports both the structure and any relevant behaviors completely. Otherwise, it becomes an empty gesture.

Where appropriate, participating managers must be trained in the criteria and techniques of measurement. Senior managers must be on hand at public award ceremonies.

TIP▶ Prepare Your Team for the Transition

You want to make it as easy and rewarding as possible for people to participate on your action team.

If you can assure your team that senior management is completely behind the action program and values the knowledge and skills that the team members are bringing to it, their fears as they make the transition out into the larger organization may be somewhat alleviated. In fact, action programs often create a new level of access and exposure to top management that can be a powerful motivator and a genuine offset to fears that a career will be sidetracked.

Combining assurances with visible incentives for delivering project results, and holding out the possibility of further rewards and opportunities for new career options, will help to cement team commitment as it moves out into the organization.

If your action team has a global makeup, relocation might require a major effort on your part—and might produce no small amount of tension—unless you can leverage internal human-resource capabilities to help handle the tasks.

Although newly selected action-team members often worry about whether their old jobs will be waiting for them when the action is completed, reintegration can be a letdown after the excitement, energy, and focus of an action.

The fact is that action-team members rarely return to their previous roles and responsibilities. Old jobs often are retooled or designed away, are filled by others, or simply no longer challenge people who have acquired new skills and experiences as part of the action.

Action-team members are more likely to assume new, key roles in the new organization or to join other action initiatives that are being launched.

Unfortunately, some team members may decide that they no longer fit into the organization and will want to leave to pursue new challenges and utilize new action-based skills and experiences.

Although such an outcome may well be part of the price of a successful action, it reinforces the importance of establishing measures and incentives to keep key team members past implementation and transition. Otherwise, continuity is threatened and critical knowledge gained during the action is lost.

Action Paths

Here's our advice on cultivating your human resources for each action path.

▶ACTION PATH Sprint

Set recognition and reward programs in a context of rapid action.

Make establishing and communicating people-deployment strategies (how people are selected from the old organization for the new) an early priority.

Speed implementation by minimizing human-resource policy and cultural shifts.

Reintegrate action resources.

Retain key action resources during and after an action's implementation.

Invest in training, so employees can upgrade their skills and move with lightning speed.

▶ACTION PATH   High Jump

Speed implementation by minimizing human-resource policy and behavioral shifts.

Establish and clearly communicate people-deployment strategies early, so employees will understand how they will be selected and treated.

Implement existing employment policies without compromising or taking shortcuts.

▶ACTION PATH   Decathlon

Take advantage of progressive human-resource policies promoting new career paths and skill development.

Build a simulation of the action's endpoint to supplement training.

Conduct early research on employment-legislation constraints in countries where the action is to be implemented.

Let local teams customize training and communication.

Leverage knowledge from one action to the next.

▶ACTION PATH   Marathon

Make the teaching of core skills to employees a progressive, ongoing activity.

Align your performance-management system with business performance and behavior.

Use human resources to maintain a focus on creating the culture the action requires with appropriate promotions.

Reinforce new behaviors with recognition and reward programs.

Questions and Answers

QUESTION: How can I identify and select the right people to fill jobs once the action is finished?

The same issues of strategy and knowledge or skill profiling apply as an action moves from initiation and analysis out into the wider organization during the definition and transition stages. The difference lies in the fact that the desired attributes are used to identify job candidates instead of team members.

Many more positions may need to be filled, of course, and decisions will have to be made about recruiting from outside the company if specific knowledge and attributes are in short supply internally.

Some things to be considered include the following:

Who will lead the selection process and make hiring decisions? (This is usually a management responsibility, with help from the human-resources department and the action team if necessary.)

Will the selection process be phased and positions filled in top-down order, thus allowing leaders to build their work units?

What positions are open, and who will be eligible to fill them? Union-represented positions, for example, often require that specific procedures be followed.

Who is eligible for voluntary severance or early retirement packages?

QUESTION: Are there different selection processes that can be used?

Yes. Consider the following approaches:

Closed selection: in which the manager of an open position selects and recruits the candidate (usually used only to put managers into key leadership positions)

Partially open selection: in which employees in a defined applicant pool apply for unfilled positions of their choosing

Fully open selection: in which everyone involved in the organization can apply for any position in the target environment

QUESTION: Some jobs are going to change and some will be lost completely as my action rolls out across the organization. I want to make sure that this is handled as smoothly as possible. What do you suggest?

If people will be displaced at varying points in time as recruitment and selection roll across the entire organization, certain issues have to be resolved—and it must be done before the action program is implemented organizationwide. Make sure your senior managers have answers to the following questions:

Will people be required to interview for jobs they already have?

If displaced people are to be given a shot at jobs opening up along the way, how will we make the process fair for those who are displaced last?

What jobs will be available for them to potentially move into?

Are there clear career paths to help place people in jobs that will help the organization now and help the employee down the road?

Will those not selected be allowed to move to another part of the organization or be offered a severance package to leave?

QUESTION: I want to make sure that there is no backlash when the jobs in the new organization are filled. Is there anything I can do to prevent it?

In organizationwide job placement, it is crucial that those chosen be recognized for their qualifications, not their connections. Equitable treatment of everyone will ensure that the survivors themselves are happier, more productive, and less fearful the next time an action rollout occurs.

QUESTION: What training issues should I be concerned with as the action rolls across the organization?

Some of the questions that you must address as you roll training out into the organization include the following:

How will eligibility for training be determined?

Who will schedule training?

Who gets trained first?

Do people have to be trained before rolling into new jobs?

How will ongoing training be funded?

What leadership attributes are important?

QUESTION: What kinds of training strategies have you run into at companies you work with?

We've had experience with a variety of training programs, of course, but one of the most comprehensive we've seen is at Bristol-Myers Squibb.

Bristol-Myers recognizes training and development as one of the elements that can make or break an action program, and its employees have access to what the company calls *Demand Management University* (DMU).

DMU is the vehicle for transferring knowledge from the company's global design team in New Jersey to the 25,000 employees worldwide who will be working with demand-management business processes once the ERP action is fully implemented.

The initial classes at DMU are focused on bringing the project team members up to speed with the skills and knowledge they will need for implementation. In the second part of the three-stage knowledge transfer, the project team will train implementation teams at the various sites, and they, in turn, will pass on the information to the end users.

Richard McIntyre, the implementation director, explains that the onsite training segment of the action program combines a formal transfer of knowledge with a support element—"someone to lean on," as he puts it—in case problems develop.

DMU also handles executive education, which typically involves leadership development, business analysis, and familiarization with the functions required to run an organization, so its audience is widespread and varied.

The company sees the acquisition of knowledge and the follow-up support as the bridge from the initial awareness stage of the action project, which is brought about through communication, to the involvement stage, and finally to the ultimate commitment stage, where all employees fully buy into the concept of demand management.

QUESTION: It seems that a lot more information-technology actions are global these days. Do they present any specific training challenges?

Yes, they certainly do. Global system implementations mean that action managers must figure out how to train thousands of users in several countries on different continents.

Here are some specific suggestions developed to meet the unique problems these implementations present:

Establish standards for training materials and process flow documents to ensure consistency.

Integrate training and development teams so that training materials incorporate development-team decisions.

Assign adequate resources to set up and maintain a training environment with sufficient global capacity.

Automate course scheduling.

Evaluate and address prerequisite needs, such as basic computer skills, before beginning training on any new software.

Assess postimplementation training requirements before a system's "go-live" date.

Determine cross-border technology capabilities and allow time for any necessary upgrading.

Where very large numbers of people need to be trained, look for ways to use computer-based training to accelerate the process.

Develop a "superuser" at each location into a trainer and local problem solver.

QUESTION: What specific things should I be concerned with as my action program moves into the transition stage?

That's a very good question—and one that is rarely asked soon enough in most actions. You need to be on top of these issues early, or risk having a monkey wrench thrown into the works as you try to integrate your action plan into the wider organization.

Specifically, you will need answers to the following questions:

What is the best organizational structure?

How should reporting relationships be set up?

What new and different skills will be needed by affected employees, and how will they be obtained?

What will be the criteria for selecting personnel?

QUESTION: What should I focus on as I plan a people-deployment strategy?

Keep people in the forefront. Use the information gathered by your human-resources personnel to address the following issues:

Redeployment of personnel into new positions with a consideration for when new technologies and facilities will be available, and supply training if needed to satisfy new skills requirements

Relocation of personnel who have accepted positions requiring transfer, including addressing any ex-pat issues that surface

Termination of employment for those taking voluntary severance or early retirement, and for employees displaced because there is no longer a fit between their capabilities and the needs of the enterprise

Management of people in transition states who can continue to contribute, including displaced employees, those taking early retirement, or transfers who have not yet been relocated but whose current jobs are no longer needed

How deployment briefings will be conducted, how the process will be communicated, and how employees can prepare

QUESTION: It's important to me that the employees displaced as part of my action program be treated with sensitivity. Can you give me any guidelines?

You've hit upon an issue that requires delicate handling, and one that produced a lot of negative comments in our survey.

Respondents criticized management's failure to acknowledge that jobs were at risk until the very last moment, as well as its failure to treat displaced employees with the dignity and respect their loyalty and years of service warranted.

How you treat those you must let go will impact on the survivors, as well. Perceptions of unfairness or poor handling may prompt surviving employees to feel sympathy for or resentment of their fellows and anxiety over their own treatment in any future action.

Another symptom is "survivor's guilt," or bad feelings about being the one who stayed rather than the one who left. (See the book, *Healing the Wounds*, by David Noer [San Francisco: Jossey-Bass Publishers, 1995], for further information on this subject.) The associated loss of trust and management credibility from these manifestations could take years to overcome.

With this reality in mind, it is critical that you create a people-deployment strategy that makes sure affected employees are apprised of their situation in one-to-one communication with their line managers. For those who are left behind, use offsite "workout programs" where full and open discussion of feelings and concerns is encouraged.

10

THE EIGHTH CHALLENGE— INTEGRATE FOR ACTION

Territorial problems yield to territorial solutions—ones that combine local fiefdoms into common ground and pull down the fences that divide backyards. Here's how to install swinging gates to let people and fresh air pass through.

When poet Robert Frost wrote "something there is that doesn't love a wall," he undoubtedly wasn't thinking of business. But business actions love walls least of all.

The walls that block action and require integration are between functions, business units, companies, and cultures.

Which type of wall do you think is highest?

If you say *cultural,* you are wrong.

Our Global Action Survey shows that, although cultural boundaries are increasingly difficult to cross, it is the functional ones that are the killers. And the bigger the actions, the higher the walls.

While we can't ignore the fact that globalization is exerting ever-greater pressure on businesses, it is still true that more turf battles erupt between people in the same building than between those on the other side of the planet. This is especially true if a business is merging or being acquired.

It's a tough world out there, with managers digging in, sandbagging, and snarling, "Tanks off my lawn."

At the least, their behavior is disruptive. In the extreme, it is civil war.

In the pages that follow, we show you how to scale the walls that loom ahead.

We start, though, with a few basics.

The four boundaries identified by our survey can, if not properly addressed, derail an action. Let's examine them—*functional, business unit, company,* and *cultural*—each in turn.

1. Functional boundaries divide work groups or departments within a company—sales from distribution, for instance.

2. Business-unit boundaries separate different lines of business within a company. At Dell Computer Corporation, for example, one business unit sells personal computers to business customers; another unit services those computers.

3. Company boundaries separate businesses within an industry— Chrysler Corporation from its suppliers, for example.

4. Cultural boundaries exist wherever value systems differ. They divide companies, countries, even cultures within countries.

The complexity of a solution is not always in direct proportion to the complexity of the problem that it attempts to solve.

Think of the theory of relativity. Many scientists spent untold hours over many years focusing on the problem of absolute motion—until Albert Einstein came up with the solution that motion is only relative to time and space: $E = mc^2$.

Although the theory of relativity is, of course, more involved than we suggest here, the point is that simple solutions, applied effectively, can and do address complex issues successfully. A complex problem doesn't always demand a complex solution.

In the pages that follow, we offer simple suggestions for solving the sometimes complex problems posed by boundaries.

You know that functions, business units, companies, and cultures create the boundaries that threaten your action. You also know that integration is the answer. Here's concrete advice on how to achieve it.

Action Tips

TIP▶ Spot the Obstacles that Reinforce Functional Boundaries

Pay attention to functional boundaries when you are reengineering processes, restructuring organizations, implementing new technologies, consolidating to achieve cost efficiencies during a merger or acquisition, or establishing new performance measures.

Examples of functional boundaries include those between purchasing and accounts payable; between sales, distribution, and warehousing; between product development, engineering, and manufacturing; and between marketing, sales, and customer service.

In each case, the boundary that must be crossed is the set of accepted behavioral norms relevant to the particular function—in a phrase, "the way things are done here."

For a finance function, the norm may involve following procedures with precise attention to detail. For a product-development function, it may be maintaining an open mind toward new ideas and innovative problem solving.

Crossing functional boundaries presents a variety of obstacles. An obvious one is dealing with the perceived threat to turf that accompanies most actions.

Whether the issue is one of power, position, or authority, the majority of turf battles are fought not with people in other companies or on the other side of the world, but with colleagues just across the hall or down a flight of stairs.

One reason for this internecine warfare is that action programs often subject people to new performance measures. These measures require employees to depend, more than was usual, on people and situations within the company but outside of their own control.

When you alter the measures used to assess your employees' performance, be mindful of the obstacles this change can throw in the face of your action.

What kind of obstacles? Well, for one thing, you may inadvertently create a perception that people did not do their jobs effectively in the past. For another, there can be increased difficulty in keeping the lines of communication open.

Crossing functional boundaries also carries with it the need for new training schemes. Employees have to be coached on how to move freely between departments in order to effectively manage a process.

▶ ────────────────────────────────────

LEARN BY EXAMPLE: **Carlton & United Breweries, Ltd.**

Carlton & United's action leaders discovered that crossing functional boundaries posed unique challenges in their three-year effort to position the company as a "lead enterprise" within Australia's food-packaging and -distribution industry.

An industry leader must be sure that it knows more than its competitors. Cognizant of that fact, Chief Executive Officer Nuno D'Aquino set out to make sure that Carlton & United was a place of constant learning.

"To be a learning organization," D'Aquino says, "you have to be able to transfer knowledge. The only way to do this is to become a team-based organization. And you have to structure your teams so that they are all mutually supportable. The biggest impediment to growth are the chimneys between different functions."

One way of breaking down the chimneys, D'Aquino found, was to encourage each team to outsource to another team any activities it didn't add value to. "By conducting this sort of in-house outsourcing," he explains, "you create dependence across functions. We now illustrate our structure by drawing three-dimensional bubbles, with a lot of miniature interlocking supports."

Carlton & United's managers also found that seemingly small gestures—such as designing the new building to incorporate an open office plan—can serve as important symbols of the need to break down functional barriers.

LEARN BY EXAMPLE: British Airways Engineering

"An inability to get through to people so that they work, and, indeed, think, cross-functionally is definitely one of the biggest barriers in pulling off major change in a business."

So says Brian Philpott, managing director for BA Engineering. Philpott led the company's effort to break down its organizational hierarchy and reconstruct its business arenas to facilitate more cross-functional cooperation.

Managers learned the hard way that acting with speed and efficiency to create a cross-functional team is a key component of action success. Why? It helps you to cross those looming functional boundaries at the earliest possible juncture, before any damage is done.

"We had laudable motives," Philpott says, "but we probably lost about six months up front managing the staffing process. I would recommend making hard, firm decisions up front, when you have a feel for about 70 to 80 percent of the project requirements, instead of waiting until you have 100 percent like we did."

Functional boundaries are usually the first barriers encountered during an action program. How they are handled will affect the entire program.

TIP▶ Spot the Obstacles that Reinforce Business-Unit Boundaries

Business-unit boundaries exist between different lines of business within the same company. These boundaries must be crossed when an action program affects two separate areas of a company's business.

Examples of different business units include brand and product lines within a consumer-products company; creative and product lines within an entertainment company; and service and product lines within a diversified corporation.

Watch out for business-unit boundaries when you are centralizing or decentralizing operations. Also take notice when implementing information, human resources, finance and accounting, strategic sourcing and purchasing systems, and other shared services to support multiple lines of business.

The obstacles that reinforce business-unit boundaries can be easy to identify but difficult to address.

The potential for barriers is increased by differences in the nature of each separate business and in the competitiveness of the individual environments. Both factors have an impact on the case for action, as well as on the sense of urgency prevailing within a business unit with regard to the action.

▶───────────────────────────────────

LEARN BY EXAMPLE: Bristol-Myers Squibb

An action commonly undertaken these days is the installation of a new information system across all units of a business. But just because these actions are common doesn't mean they are easy to carry out.

Bristol-Myers Squibb recently began a SAP installation that stretched across all divisions of its supply chain. The company opted for a global design rather than one particular to a specific group, such as pharmaceuticals, medical devices, or consumer products. And its biggest challenge lay in carrying out this design.

As project director Dana Cooper explains, the company took great pains to maintain the global focus by recruiting people for project teams from all segments of its business around the world.

"We borrowed executives from the respective divisions, thereby ensuring that each division had a vested interest in the design," Cooper says. "This created unity between the divisions. When you're working on an integrated problem, you can't really segregate divisions, so we are all very interrelated. It also ensured that the project was not viewed as a U.S.-centric project."

LEARN BY EXAMPLE: **Braun**

When Braun launched a reengineering project that involved major cost cutting as well as the introduction of a new software system, top managers decided to first pilot the action in only a few operations. That way, they could figure out what kind of timetable was reasonable and be on guard for potentially troublesome issues when the time came for an organizationwide implementation.

From the start, managers knew that to successfully retool business processes and introduce standardized software on a worldwide basis, the company would have to work hard to keep an open flow of communication across all the different business units. One technique advocated by action leaders was a system that rotated managers through each of the different units at six-month intervals.

What Joseph Vanicek, executive director for central Europe, describes as "a lot of coaching and explaining" also went into the effort to make sure that a common understanding about the company's objectives prevailed across the various units.

"We had an organization where each of our subsidiaries was very independent," Vanicek points out, "so we had to make it quite clear that it was not our intention to standardize everything, even though we knew that we would have to let go of some of that independence."

◄

TIP▶ **Spot the Obstacles That Reinforce Company Boundaries**

Enterprise boundaries are crossed when an action program requires cooperation on any level by two different companies within the same industry.

Take heed of company boundaries when you are setting up a partnership, joint venture, or strategic alliance; introducing a supply-chain initiative; or implementing a merger or acquisition that may require a modification of corporate culture.

Invariably, crossing an enterprise boundary involves changing both the number of employees and the nature of their roles and loyalties.

Potential obstacles include the human responses triggered by these situations. Fear of a shift in the balance of power, fear of the loss of a job, and fear of increased codependencies with "outsiders" are not uncommon.

There can also be resistance to building new relationships with people in companies that once were, and maybe still are, suppliers, customers, or even competitors. Watch out as well for any resistance born of the not-invented-here mind-set.

▶─────────────────────────────────────

LEARN BY EXAMPLE: **Nynex**

When Nynex merged with Bell Atlantic in 1995 to form a $28-billion telecommunications company, the cross-enterprise integration challenges facing top management were substantial. A pervading sense of displacement coupled with job-related stress threatened the merger's success.

"The issue to be dealt with in this kind of program is primarily one of trust," explains Judy Habberkorn, president of public and operator services. "When you are merging companies and putting in new leadership, there are a lot of questions like, 'Who are these new people and what do they believe?' "

Seeking to ensure employee support for, and participation in, the merged organization, the company adopted a results-oriented compensation system. It worked.

"If you weren't going to be able to achieve your results, you weren't going to be paid," Habberkorn says. "People pretty much had to start working together right off the bat. There were no special incentives, but that was enough."

TIP▶ Spot the Obstacles That Reinforce Cultural Boundaries

Look for cultural boundaries when you are aligning processes between operations in different countries, combining or aligning organizational structures between operations in different countries or regions, or combining or aligning processes or organizational structures between businesses that have different leadership styles.

Cultural boundaries arise because of different value systems. And value differences can be just as broad between people working in two separate departments located in the same building as between people residing in two separate countries located on different continents.

If you assume that the trend toward globalization of businesses creates even more complex cultural barriers, you are mistaken. Globalization may, indeed, be putting more strain on organizations, but the boundary issues haven't really changed.

In fact, the need to address cultural boundaries is usually recognized and readily accepted in global situations. But when the boundary being crossed is as narrow as that between two functions in the same department, the significance of culture may be overlooked.

What kind of obstacles confront an action program that spans cultural boundaries?

When the boundaries are geographic (those involving country or regional value differences), barriers include different operating models, different levels of respect for authority, different approaches to time, different needs for spatial interaction, different levels of comfort with ambiguity, different attitudes about the importance of work relationships, and different business and regulatory environments.

Overcoming these barriers generally requires different styles of communication, and may call for multiple language skills to facilitate both information sharing and relationship building. It also requires training in cultural differences.

▶
―――――――――――――――――――――――――――――――――――――

Learn by Example: SkyChefs, Inc.

When SkyChefs bought Caterair, its largest competitor, managers assumed that the biggest challenge was to incorporate SkyChefs' proven cycle-time reduction (CTR) process into the newly acquired kitchens.

Eighteen months after the acquisition, the implementation of CTR was on schedule everywhere except Europe. What SkyChefs' managers had failed to consider in designing the action program were the cultural differences between the U.S. and European arms of the organization. Faulty assumptions had been made based on the U.S. rollout.

Specifically, SkyChefs' management realized soon after the project began that 40 percent of its European leadership was incapable of driving the action. They possessed neither the skills nor the behavior to own and lead the action locally.

As Joe Primavera, the vice president for human resources, explains, "Coming up against these cultural boundaries meant we had to step backwards, realign our objectives, and start strengthening the management team by reassessing the required skills."

The problem could have been avoided, Primavera believes, had the action team identified the cultural barriers before the implementation process began. The mistake lay in thinking that SkyChefs could leverage its success in the United States into similar gains around the world.

The solution for SkyChefs was to relocate responsibility.

"We've made it a European program, with European leadership and ownership," says Primavera. "The action program has to be owned locally, directed locally, controlled locally, and resourced locally."

When the cultural boundaries are not based on geography, such as those stemming from differences in functions, business units, or enterprises, they still need to be addressed in much the same way.

In confronting obstacles that may include standards of behavior, measures of success, styles of leadership, and degree of loyalty among employees, communication is once again the key.

Managers must understand and articulate the fundamental goals of the action.

LEARN BY EXAMPLE: **Barclaycard**

Barclaycard's director of operations, Linda Walton, told us that the company's House of Pillars image (see Figure 8.2) developed out of an effort to integrate the five goals that drive its action program into a single expression of value.

At a team meeting, she says, "we were trying to picture how all of our programs—motivating people, delivering the budget, excelling in our customer service, installing a new technology, and developing our brand—fit in with the business as a whole.

"What that resulted in was a house, with the roof as the mission statement, and those five key objectives as the pillars. The foundation would have to be built by people working to achieve those objectives.

"We now measure everything according to its contribution to building and sustaining this house," Walton said.

Action Paths

Here's our advice on overcoming barriers for each action path.

▶ACTION PATH   Sprint

Determine the extent to which the action will cross cultural, business, and functional lines by weighing the importance of its doing so against the inevitable added time.

▶ACTION PATH   High Jump

Spot and avoid the duplication of effort that often results from integration. Save time and money by doing things once.

▶ACTION PATH   Decathlon

Launch the action in one area of the organization to jump-start the action team's effort businesswide.

Promote top-down acceptance of the business case from top management at headquarters to local country management.

▶ACTION PATH   Marathon

Make sure that the organization recognizes and values the integration behaviors of teamwork, process working, networking, and international collaboration.

Topple functional barriers by striking first at top-team structure and membership.

Encourage and reward network development.

Use measures to drive behavior over the long term.

Reward not just for producing results, but for developing ways to achieve them.

Questions and Answers

QUESTION: Will my action hit all four barriers, or is one more common than the others?

Every action will run smack into at least one—if not all—of our four boundaries. At the moment, though, the walls that separate functions are the most frequently encountered—and the most difficult to climb.

But problems associated with cultural boundaries are on the rise. In fact, our survey data and field work indicate that action managers will soon spend the majority of their efforts on bridging cultural boundaries.

QUESTION: How can incentives help cross boundaries?

Incentives are a powerful integration tool.

We recommend creating process- or program-based personal- and business-performance measures that cut across boundaries. Apply them to everyone in the organization.

To ensure that the performance goals are met, link appropriate incentives to these measures.

If you are trying to get people to cooperate in different ways across boundaries but you don't change the schemes for assessing the results of their attempts, or if you don't make it personally meaningful for them to operate in that way, you won't be getting away from "business as usual."

Remember, what gets measured gets managed. And what gets managed gets done.

QUESTION: How can my team help eliminate barriers?

Set up expectations that action-team members will become experts in all areas of the program, instead of just maintaining the expertise they possessed when the action began.

Organize each individual's roles and responsibilities to reflect this expectation. Also, facilitate additional learning. The entire team needs to understand the action's perspectives and issues from front to back.

QUESTION: Involving people from both sides of any given boundary is slow and expensive. Do I have to?

Yes.

Avoid the mistake made by one multi-billion-dollar company we worked with: During the first nine months of this company's action-program design, a key executive was kept in the dark about the proposed action. Yet activities under her direct control accounted for half the scope the strategic action was designed to address.

This failure to employ even minimal integration techniques created tremendous resistance. It was overcome only through compromises that significantly lessened the impact of the action.

Operate from a solid knowledge base. Involve the right people at the right time.

Also, if you plan to roll out your action in several countries, make sure that all country representatives participate in the design.

The contribution of these representatives is essential to determine different methods of action implementation. Also vital is their input on legislation and working practices peculiar to each country.

QUESTION: Will boundary issues change across the life of my action?

Yes.

Recognize that your action will have a different effect on each of your operations, and that boundary issues may differ, as well.

Size, scope, complexity, duration—there are multiple variables in any action program. And the confluence of these variables will play a part in the boundaries you encounter at different points along the way.

The only way to account for these differences during the planning stage is by remaining flexible. Be prepared to deal with boundary issues if and when they become apparent.

QUESTION: Will I encounter organizational-culture obstacles?

Almost certainly.

Almost every boundary an action crosses will be accompanied by a cultural obstacle. Multisite implementations involve crossing as many cultural boundaries as do multicountry rollouts.

Understand how different team functions create different business cultures.

Above all, don't assume that because an initiative works one way in one area, it will work similarly in another. Trust us, it won't.

Bear in mind what is particularly meaningful to the culture of your team, and structure your activities and performance measures accordingly.

11

THE NINTH CHALLENGE—
WIRE FOR ACTION

*Don't worry, we won't try to make you an overnight technical
systems expert. We will make you an expert at spotting the
issues that snag major information-technology action
programs, then we will suggest ways to deal with them.*

Information technology was supposed to put us in the fast lane. So why
are we stuck in traffic? The headlines tell the tale.

Item: Projects involving the installation of new technology cost
twice their budgeted amount and take three times longer than esti-
mated to complete.

Item: One-third of all company-sponsored software-development
projects are canceled and abandoned.

Item: Half of all information-technology projects promise big benefits and greater functionality—then don't deliver.

Item: Failed application projects cost businesses more than $80 bil-
lion annually in the United States alone.

Our Global Action Survey tells the tale, too.

More than 35 percent of our respondents said they didn't have enough
time to plan, design, construct, and implement information technology.

Some 25 percent complained that the systems they installed didn't live up to their promise.

It is a tidal wave of scandal, a tsunami of bad news. And, if you are planning a business action—and we mean *any* action—it is heading right at you.

How can you stop it? Read this chapter and wire for action.

To begin, a few key distinctions.

Sometimes, information technology *is* the action. Sometimes, information technology *supports* the action.

What's the difference?

The implementation of enterprise resource planning (ERP) software is an example of technology as action. The installation of a bar-code system to speed up a process is an example of technology that supports action.

These distinctions aside, information technology affects virtually every corner of a business in action—that is, every unit that is restructured, every process that is reengineered, and, by extension, every employee who is engaged therein.

It is hard enough to install new technology and make it run correctly. But action managers must do more.

They must integrate the new system into their overall action. Only then can they determine how the organization will operate, deliver value to its customers, and stay competitive.

Consider the case of Progressive Corporation, the fifth-largest automobile insurer in the United States. The company is striving to become the country's number-three car insurer by the year 2000—and it is likely to succeed.

Technology plays a central role in nearly all business actions at Progressive, especially the reengineering of processes.

Progressive, a high-risk niche insurer based in Cleveland, Ohio, has broadened its reach by simultaneously cutting costs and boosting customer service. These accomplishments were made possible by information technology.

Its Immediate Response claims service, for example, provides on-the-spot claims settlements within hours, sometimes minutes, of an accident. A policyholder's call to an 800 number summons an Immediate Response claims representative—equipped with a cellular phone and a laptop computer—to the scene.

The representative can file a report—and, if necessary, alert police, tow trucks, or repair facilities—on the spot. He or she can even cut a check to pay the claimant.

Another example of how Progressive has used information technology to achieve competitive advantage is its innovative Internet site. Policyholders can now check their account status online, make payments, access information about their policies, and view their policy contracts.

"We're constantly changing," says Peter Lewis, the company's chairman and chief executive officer. Under his stewardship, Progressive's annual revenues grew from $23.5 million in 1965 to $3.4 billion in 1996.

Progressive got technology right.

How can you, the action manager, get technology right?

The key, we argue, is to avoid turning information-technology solutions into information-technology problems. In the remainder of this chapter, we show you how.

Action Tips

TIP▶ Delay is Deadly to Technology Projects

Time isn't on your side. Information technology gets faster all the time, but its installation is fraught with delays.

Sometimes it seems that whatever technology you decide to implement will be out of date by the time your fingers touch a keyboard. Sometimes it seems that you are chasing a moving target and are always falling further behind.

And you are.

The problem runs deeper, however, than trying to keep up with the latest software or more powerful computer processors. A change in hardware and software is often part of, or requires some larger change in, the way people or processes work—this dissonance can stop an action cold.

Item: You install new information technology to help your customer-order department fill orders faster. But the actual time expended isn't reduced at all, because employees still have to check inventory by hand.

Item: You install a superfast computer system to enable people to work more rapidly. But they don't, because the culture itself hasn't changed to support and reward faster action, speedier decisions, and streamlined processes.

Action is impossible if the underlying technology is in a constant state of flux. What's more, unsettled conditions fuel the skepticism of those within the organization who believe that the technology solution won't deliver anyway.

All too often, they're right. If technology benefits promised within six months don't pan out within two years, top-level sponsorship of the implementation is bound to take a number of hits. And the project languishes in unexploited potential.

A global consumer-products company with which we are familiar, for example, envisioned an extensive array of technologically driven capabilities that it planned to unveil stage by stage. But leaders, primed to see the system in all its glory, became disillusioned when the early unveilings fell short of the press they had been given.

A more serious problem befell a company that made future pricing deals based on benefits it *thought* would be delivered by its new ERP system. The benefits didn't materialize in time, and the company went out of business.

TIP▶ Even Planned Delay Can Be Deadly

We ran into a situation a few years back where a major multinational corporation decided to install an ERP system, business unit by business unit. *Each* implementation was slated to take between two and three years.

By stretching out the lead times and allowing a high degree of divisional independence, the company virtually guaranteed that problems would present themselves—and they did.

About three and a half years into the separate implementations, skyrocketing expenses forced the divisions to come to the corporate parent for more money. The budget problems were nothing new, but the implementation structure kept the shortfalls hidden until the overruns totaled hundreds of millions of dollars.

The board, having lost track of the projects, was left to wonder what the objectives had been in the first place. It hardly mattered, though, because the business atmosphere—in fact, the company itself—had changed so much that the original rationale was no longer valid anyway.

When an action program affecting significant portions of a business spans years rather than months, the likelihood also increases that the company will initiate other action programs along the way.

And what happens then? You guessed it. More delay.

One company we know began implementing a corporatewide technology project to define its data needs only to have its managers shift their attention to the development of standards for recording and reporting that data.

Another company instituted a separate program to revise the number of levels in the corporate reporting structure while it was in the middle of designing a major technology project.

Yet another hired an outside group to help revise its sales and marketing planning at the very moment that system functionality was being designed.

Each of these companies experienced technology implementation delays. At best, the new programs are a temporary distraction; at worst, they can require much reworking of the original vision and execution strategy.

▶

LEARN BY EXAMPLE: Siemens Medical Systems

Siemens Medical Systems, a division of Munich-based Siemens AG, produces X-ray machines, ultrasound and magnetic resonance systems, and computer tomography. Facing heavy competition from U.S. and Japanese companies, Siemens Medical decided that it needed to replace its 25-year-old information system—to which people in the company had become quite attached—with a SAP system.

"We couldn't improve our worldwide supply chain," program manager Olaf Reiher explains, "without completely throwing away old tools, including our legacy system. To change people's thinking, we had to change systems first."

At the same time, however, parent company Siemens AG was beginning its own actions, which had a significant impact on the corporate culture and business processes.

Reiher admits that changing the technology program in a separate effort was not an ideal approach. "But we learned quickly to coordinate these activities in a special program group of business unit leaders," he says.

◄

TIP▶ Understand the Real Source of Technology Delay

The dangers of delayed information-technology implementation are easily imagined, but until now, the root cause of the problem was not clearly understood.

As Figure 11.1 illustrates, the traditional way that many managers think about designing, developing, installing, and maintaining an information-technology solution falls into four distinct stages, each relatively discrete.

What's wrong with this picture?

For one thing, the thinking is truly "inside the box," to paraphrase a cliché.

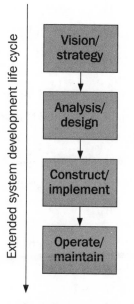

Figure 11.1 Misconceived life cycle of system development.

The diagram suggests that, after completing one step, action managers need only move to the next, then the next, hopscotching their way to the fully operational, originally envisioned system. But life is rarely so neat.

Visions and strategies do not stand still. Projects change even as they are being created. New technology appears, tempting action managers to reconsider their original strategy and draw up new plans. During implementation, disconnects—both literal and figurative—are found between the tool (the information system itself) and the work it was designed to do.

And what happens then? You know. More delay as development plans are adapted and readapted to reflect an environment in motion.

How can you solve this dilemma?

TIP▶ Envision Your Projects in Increments

We suggest that projects be envisioned not in terms of *all* that is required to bring about the ultimate end result, but rather in terms of what can be implemented in manageable increments and then expanded upon in succeeding stages.

Figure 11.2 presents a hypothetical project as it develops in six-month increments over a two-year time frame (Y1/H1 = the first half of the first year of the project).

After performing the requisite analysis, managers direct the design and construction of an information technology system in incremental parts at six-month intervals, with an eye toward designing and building on work in progress.

Compare this to the old way, in which the whole system is based on an initial, static vision that becomes further and further removed from reality as the project progresses.

Which makes more sense?

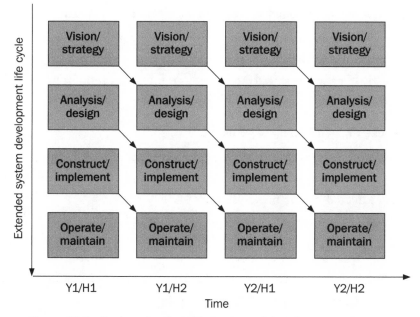

Figure 11.2   System developed in incremental parts.

By continually creating visions that build on what is proposed to be implemented, while, at the same time, installing the previously envisioned pieces, the action manager shortens the life cycle and makes sure that the overall project stays on track to its desired end.

TIP▶ Help Leaders Make Informed Decisions

Successfully managing the long lead time for an information-technology project obviously requires serious planning and commitment, especially from top managers who themselves may not be around to see the project's conclusion.

If leadership changes occur during an action, action managers need to help new leaders make quick, responsible, and informed decisions about whether to stop a project, change its direction, or continue to support it as originally conceived.

TIP▶ Help Workers Adjust to New Technology and New Roles

At the same time, action managers have to help frontline workers accustom themselves to the new technology and new roles, in part through training. But, as we've said, training is certainly no cure-all for the problems attending the installation of a new system.

TIP▶ Use Phased Technology Rollouts

A phased technology rollout can be useful, especially if it can demonstrate the overall benefit to the organization and to the people whose jobs are affected by the new system.

Rollouts also allow people to see early on what possibilities lie in store.

▶────────────────────────────────────

LEARN BY EXAMPLE: Bristol-Myers Squibb

Bristol-Myers Squibb, for instance, spent $250,000 to create a sample ERP installation so that employees could see the future.

It also created two pilot programs—in Greensboro, North Carolina, and Swords, Ireland—to achieve true integration of the information technology with business processes—all the way from forecasting through cost accounting, procurement, manufacturing, quality control, and other parts of the virtual supply chain.

All-at-once actions—those that take place suddenly and have wide-reaching effects throughout the organization—may require longer information-technology lead times as needed refinements are made.

Even though the implementation risks are greater—because a lot of money is invested in a system that may not deliver what was promised—a short schedule has advantages. It forces everyone to respond to an imminent crisis and it quickly shifts values and expectations.

Dana Cooper at Bristol-Myers Squibb explains that action managers there considered such an approach but rejected it because it was not right for the company's situation:

When some people install ERP systems, they sometimes install only one or two modules, and in essence they can accomplish the effects of a big bang. In our case, however, the scale of the project called for replacing almost all of the systems at a manufacturing location, and that's as close to a big bang as we want to get.

Action Paths

Here's our advice on overcoming information-technology challenges for each action path.

▶**ACTION PATH** Sprint

Restrict information-technology project scope, customization, and new developments to assure timely and cost-efficient delivery of added benefits.

Reduce development times by reviewing rapid prototyping approaches to system development.

▶**ACTION PATH** High Jump

Set up an information-technology task force to make an early assessment of the current system and how it relates to the needs of the action.

Recognize that the first information-technology priority is business continuity and not systems improvement.

▶**ACTION PATH** Decathlon

Review all cutting-edge information-technology solutions.

Make sure momentum is sustained after new technology is introduced.

Reconcile dependencies between information technology and all new processes.

Take advantage of longer time scales to consider innovative information-technology solutions.

Involve the information-technology department in the earliest stages of your action so as to facilitate the interlinking of systems.

▶ACTION PATH   **Marathon**

Pilot new information technology extensively in two locations before rollout.

Use live demonstrations to sell the new system.

Anticipate local stress when integrating with other areas' technology.

Defuse efforts to retain old systems.

Deliver information technology on longer lead times to help dispel any management assumptions that it will solve a multitude of organizational issues.

Questions and Answers

QUESTION: What are some of the potential pitfalls in instituting the technology component of an action program?

Try not to promise what you can't deliver. Raising unrealistic expectations can lead to disappointment and plummeting morale.

In some instances, high-flown promises are made to convince the board of directors to commit funds for needed information-technology actions. Or sometimes a project grows more complex as people request more sophisticated information-technology functions—a situation called *scope creep.*

Although scope creep bedevils many of the multinational organizations we surveyed, sometimes it's the stakeholders' perspective that changes, not the project. Then disappointment sets in as the project takes shape and its limits become clear.

Engaging in major actions is a learning process. Emphasize to stakeholders the necessity of remaining open and flexible as the journey progresses.

Specifically, the action team should undertake due diligence. Study other companies that have successfully completed similar information-technology programs. Discover what trade-offs they've had to make, and learn whether the system met objectives.

Use the information you uncover to keep expectations in line. In fact, you may need to manage expectations down so that you can meet or exceed them.

One global entertainment company we surveyed controlled expectations by presenting an incremental technology implementation plan with a five-year timetable. Nobody was led to expect overnight miracles.

This strategy works well if the system can accommodate later add-ons, if the project calls for the gradual incorporation of specific functions or departments, or if improvements in one process are needed before alterations can be made in others.

QUESTION: Is technology the most important ingredient for success in the global economy?

No. Technology is not a cure-all. If an organization has problems elsewhere—structure, personnel, core processes, value proposition, competitive position, and so on—a new system probably won't solve them.

A dysfunctional process is still dysfunctional, regardless of whether it's automated. Competitive advantage comes from continuously improved processes and people.

QUESTION: There's so much dazzling technology out there. How can I determine what's right for my company?

First of all, take a deep breath and don't be taken in by all the razzmatazz.

Modern-day equivalents to old-time snake-oil salesmen will swear that their applications can have you gushing black ink in a matter of months. Politely show them the door.

Then undertake a methodical examination of your objectives and current capabilities.

What is the company trying to accomplish? A larger return on investment? Greater customer satisfaction? Reduced costs? More control over inventory and manufacturing processes?

Could information technology help it reach these goals? (This is a crucial question. Think long and hard about your answer.)

If you answer yes, call in reputable experts and determine what is available and applicable.

Action managers must also weigh the enormous costs of technology against the potential benefits. They have to be clear about what a specific technology can *actually* deliver as opposed to what proponents *claim* it can deliver.

For example, Efficient Consumer Response (ECR) may process orders faster, but it doesn't change the order process itself. You may gain a few seconds, but if you still need a human being to check prices and inventory, ECR won't necessarily deliver a perceptible benefit to the customer who is placing the order.

QUESTION: How important is scheduling when it comes to implementing technology?

Careful scheduling is crucial. Too often, an inflexible deadline drives an information-technology project, forcing a system to "go live" even though everyone knows it's not ready.

Be wary of setting unrealistic or rigid deadlines. You'll end up with a flawed system that leaves employees gasping.

At a global video distribution company, for example, such extreme emphasis was placed on "slamming the system in" that, in the end, the project failed. Implementation issues given short shrift because of time pressures eventually came back to haunt the organization.

QUESTION: Many of the leaders at my company resist the latest technology advances. How can I convince them of the technology's worth?

That's a tough question.

Many top managers tend to look on information-technology projects as a sinkhole of expenditures. Change the information technology, they argue, and you automatically have to retrain the workforce to use it, hire new systems experts, and invest millions in the hardware and software. And then, by the time the show is up and running, the performance is inadequate or outdated.

The truth is that information-technology systems *are* high-risk. Managers arguing for technology investment should not try to sugarcoat the cost or complexity.

While acknowledging the magnitude of the challenge, action managers must stress the potential rewards and work to minimize the roadblocks. The organization must be prepared to integrate the action at the highest levels.

For instance, does the company's chief information officer report directly to the chief executive officer and actively participate in the highest echelon of the company's structure? Does the company's strategy incorporate the current or future system?

Make leaders aware of the demands they are making on the information-technology staff. Are the staffers being asked to provide solutions that cannot be supported by current capabilities?

Creating buy-in at the top is one of the action manager's toughest jobs—and one of the most crucial.

Educate your leadership about the implications and benefits of various solutions. Start regular dialogues between the information-technology staff and the leadership.

QUESTION: How important is training when instituting a new system?

No one would argue that training isn't important. But managers often rely too heavily on training as *the* answer to every problem associated with an information-technology system.

Further complicating matters is the fact that many companies—especially large ones with global workforces—underestimate the cost of training. When costs start to escalate, they scramble to scale back, often in all the wrong places.

We recently encountered a company that, in a misguided attempt to save money, decided to develop its own in-house training without suitable support.

The result: longer training (9 to 10 days versus the usual 4) at a higher cost, both in dollars and in work time lost. Also, the knowledge-retention rate was minimal because the overall program stretched to nearly four months and didn't provide a way for early trainees to practice and refine their skills.

Another common shortcoming of training is the inability to address individual issues related to the new workload. We all learn at different rates and have widely disparate attitudes and aptitudes, so it is difficult to provide customized training in a few sessions.

Although coaching one-on-one or in small groups is time-consuming, we believe it is invaluable for helping employees to grow comfortable with and learn to master a new system. This tool also provides managers with critical feedback about what does and doesn't work in the new system where it really counts—in action.

QUESTION: Can I apply our system worldwide?

No. You can *never* get all processes and systems across a worldwide supply chain to operate in an identical and complementary fashion. Although some companies view global commonality as a good idea, the fact is that the limitations of a global design far outweigh any perceived benefits.

For all the talk of the global economy, managers must recognize that they are dealing with different markets, customs, languages, and regulatory environments. Global standardization may well be impossible.

If nothing else, it will wreak havoc with your implementation schedule. It makes much more sense to think in terms of global strategy while implementing technology based on local realities.

What can readily become global, though, is information—knowing, for example, how much of a product is sold where and at what price. By focusing on a system that delivers valuable facts, a manager eliminates the risk of building a gargantuan system (at a gargantuan cost) that will take forever to implement and will delay the entire action program.

QUESTION: What steps can I take to ensure that my information-technology vendors deliver what they promise?

Vendors often make claims that can't be substantiated. In the case of long-term action projects, it is tempting to be swayed by assurances that updates will solve any shortcomings.

Installing updates in the midst of a project, however, can be dangerous: Not only is there the risk of software incompatibilities, but the project itself is almost sure to be lengthened, especially when it involves hundreds, if not thousands, of employees.

Adaptec ran into the problem of unsubstantiated vendor claims when it discovered that its new ERP installation didn't have the mission-critical ability to track product lots. It came close to halting the project, moving forward only when the software manufacturer agreed to cofund a real-time research and development effort to design and build in the needed functionality.

Insist on interviewing previous buyers of the product about their experiences. If you can't validate vendor promises, then think about buying elsewhere.

Drive a tough bargain. Have the vendor run the software through specific transactions that are applicable to your needs. Insist that the people who run the demonstrations be part of your implementation team, because the team's skill sets have a lot to do with how much functionality a product delivers. Demand guarantees of performance.

12

THE TENTH CHALLENGE — REENERGIZE FOR ACTION

Success primes people to meet new challenges when the trumpet of action sounds again.

The crowd is cheering. The flags are waving. Your troops are marching off to implement your action program.

Time passes. Reports from the front say the enemy is engaged, morale is high, and you will have victory any day.

Then more time passes. Reports are few. A handful of recruits go AWOL. They are shell shocked and battle weary.

An action leader calls from the front. "We're fogged in out here," he says, "low on rations. We're coming home."

Wait! How can this be?

The fact is, an action program isn't self-renewing, as our Global Action Survey shows. It obeys the law of entropy, which, when enforced to the letter, relegates the universe to inertness.

Is there any hope at all for reenergizing your action program?

Yes, because action is like personal fitness: The more you work out, the fitter you get.

Does fitness trump entropy? Grab some dumbbells, read this chapter, and find out.

Action Tips

TIP▶ Understand Why Fatigue Strikes

Our Global Action Survey revealed five major sources of action fatigue:

1. *Action overload.* When faced with multiple initiatives, action managers, their teams, and even entire organizations are so overwhelmed by the sheer number of projects that they simply shut down.

2. *Inattentive leaders.* Without clear direction, support, and inspiration from senior executives, many actions grind to a halt.

3. *Overemphasis.* If the business focus is entirely on an action, day-to-day functions—like customer service, employee development, or recruitment—can break down.

4. *Depression and anger.* Without a way to express their concerns and dissatisfaction, people become depressed, angry, and fatigued. Action fatigue in this case is more mental than physical, but early signs of the problem may be evident in people's inability to focus and take an action project seriously.

5. *Slow implementation.* When an action proceeds at a snail's pace, or fails to demonstrate tangible accomplishments, fatigue is sure to ensue.

TIP▶ Combat Action Overload

Just as people who eat gargantuan lunches find it difficult to stay awake in the afternoon, managers beset by too many initiatives suffer the enervating effects of fatigue. But how many is *too* many?

The answer to the inevitable *quantity* question depends, of course, on *quality*—the kind of action you are trying to implement, the kind of people you have assigned to the project, the kind of resources available to them, the kind of training they receive, and so on.

In some companies, two major actions would be too many. In others, as many as 20 or 30 projects may be humming along unaffected by the others.

Dana Cooper, project director at Bristol-Myers Squibb, notes, for example, that his SAP-implementation action, which affected 30 sites over four years, was only one among four major ongoing actions at the company.

One out of every three companies we surveyed experienced fatigue brought on by the perception that they had taken on too much, too fast. In each case, multiple projects were running simultaneously.

"We have been sold off, privatized, and then sold off again," says an action manager in the United Kingdom. "Our employees are all a bit shell shocked and probably can't take much more."

▶
Learn by Example: SkyChefs, Inc.

At SkyChefs, Chief Executive Officer Michael Kay argues forcefully against trying to do too much at one time.

"It has to do with the capacity of the organization to change," he says. "At some point, there has to be a critical discussion of how many new things people can learn, and then develop the skills to put them into practice.

"You end up giving people more than they can eat and digest," Kay concludes, "and then you come back and have to reteach." Simply put, overloading leads to underperforming.

It is, of course, not always true that action reduces an organization's capacity to take on more action. In fact, as Adaptec and other high-tech companies illustrate, if an organization thrives on sudden moves, one action can spawn many others.

A number of Adaptec people noted that the company's recent action had increased their appetite and confidence for the next one.

TIP▶ Bring Inattentive Leaders to Attention with Balanced Communication

Few things can sap the strength of an action program sooner than the perception that top leaders are lukewarm to it.

What's the antidote? In a word, *communication*. But, as with everything, balance is key.

Sending too few messages causes people to forget that an action program is still going on; sending too many messages, especially if they all sound alike, causes people to tune out and ignore the call to action.

LEARN BY EXAMPLE: Neiman Marcus and Adaptec

Leaders at Neiman Marcus first tried to highlight the company's reengineering effort by means of a separate newsletter to stakeholders. They abandoned this strategy after they decided that they needed to make the effort seem more mainstream.

The solution they came up with was to incorporate information about the action in the company's magazine.

Adaptec leaders solved the communication problem by organizing a forum and inviting approximately 75 top-tier managers. The forum featured a keynote address by the noted Massachusetts Institute of Technology professor, Dr. John Donovan.

At this kickoff, Adaptec leaders spelled out the business case for their latest action and announced the appointment of Jim Schmidt, a respected member of the company, to direct the action project.

Learn by Example: Adaptec, Inc.

Managing the interplay of regular business processes and the demands of an action program is a common cause of fatigue. The stress apparent in Gina Gloski's voice is a clear sign of fatigue and frustration.

Gloski, the director of manufacturing at Adaptec, was promised that she would need to spend only 25 percent of her time on the Apex project. But Gloski says she actually devotes as much as 60 percent of her efforts to Apex.

Colleague Delores Marciel, vice president of procurement, tells much the same story:

> Officially, I allocate 25 percent of my time [to Apex], but it ends up being much more than that.
>
> You can't say that you're going to carve up your day and give an hour here, two hours there. It just doesn't work that way.
>
> My entire life is spent working with the suppliers or with engineering. This is not a procurement project, and Apex is not a supply-chain issue. I've got this dedicated team that can keep focused on the project, and they don't have to worry about keeping the business alive and working with the day-to-day issues.

Gloski and Marciel illustrate an important point about integrating an action project into the daily routine of a business: Although some team members may enjoy the luxury of being able to give undivided attention to an action, many others will have to play dual roles.

Like Marciel and Gloski at Adaptec, some people must divide their time between managing an action and business as usual. Although it is impossible in many cases to precisely quantify the number of hours they devote to each endeavor, they cannot afford to put up a sign proclaiming, "Closed for Reengineering."

◀

TIP▶ Establish New Performance Measures

In our experience, one of the best techniques for overcoming overemphasis is to establish new performance measures. Old measures—for example, number or amount of sales—simply guarantee that old behaviors will remain in place and even grow stronger.

A sales force accustomed to compensation based on commission, for instance, will resist any action that threatens this method of calculating pay. The threat becomes more pronounced when an employee is asked to serve two masters, taking on responsibilities associated with an action as well as performing day-to-day job duties.

▶───────────────────────────────

LEARN BY EXAMPLE: Adaptec, Inc.

Recognizing the risks associated with committing to an action program, Adaptec took special pains to adequately compensate its employees.

Paul Hansen, chief financial officer, explains:

> We engaged human resources people, then designed reward systems that supported people stepping out of their normal career paths and engaging in this large-scale project.

The new compensation system, Hansen goes on, allows employees associated with the Apex project to receive up to 30 percent of salary in bonuses. Employees "are eligible for a 50 percent greater bonus by being part of the Apex project than they would be within their normal functions," he says.

Other, noncompensation measures can also be effective.

LEARN BY EXAMPLE: Bank Corporation

At Bank Corporation, the finance sector made sure that only true savings to shareholders would be counted toward its cost-savings objective. Intent on not allowing any cost-saving shell games, finance managers developed a rigorous system of measures, stipulating that only savings in personnel expenses would be counted.

To accomplish its objective, Bank Corporation managers created a database with every finance employee's name and salary, then determined that only those employees who truly and completely left the finance division (for example, in a transfer to another area of the bank or to a job outside the bank) would be removed from the database.

In addition, the work those employees performed in the finance department had to disappear, too. But any claim of eliminated work that was not supported by a reduction in employment levels could not be counted.

Managers also had to explain what happened to the work those finance employees had done. Only in this way could the division demonstrate that the money and effort were actually saved, as opposed to just being hidden among other expenses.

◀

TIP▶ Watch for Depression and Anger

Action teams that have been running hard for a year or more to reach the first milestone of implementation may need some time together away from the site to rejuvenate themselves, express their feelings about the project, and rebuild that sense of enthusiastic cooperation with which they began.

If team members have no one else to blame for the organization's poor performance or lack of progress toward implementing an action program, they blame themselves. Anger suppressed or unspoken turns into guilt, and guilt engenders depression.

As Figure 12.1 suggests, the typical curve shows that performance rises just before the action, then drops off during the project, often bottoming out several months or years into the program.

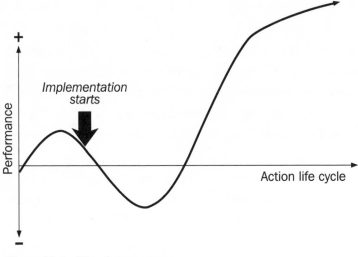

Figure 12.1   The change curve.

In truth, there may be several of these valleys over the course of long-term projects before performance begins to rise steadily, and almost predictably, toward the success targets the company has established.

TIP▶ Make Retreats a Regular Occurrence

Our experience shows that one session or retreat is hardly sufficient to cope with this problem. Often, teams require frequent meetings—weekly, if not daily—to keep focused and bridge any divisions they may be experiencing.

Even when the workload was at its heaviest, British Airways Engineering teams met in a series of planned sessions to air their concerns and keep themselves focused on the project.

TIP▶ Beat Slow Implementation with Appropriate Time Horizons

Actions that take a long time are particularly susceptible to fatigue, which can impair judgment and cast a pall over a high-spirited team. Our data supports the notion that projects lasting longer than two years suffer from a loss of focus among workers.

It is imperative, therefore, that you use an appropriate time horizon. In other words, if you anticipate that the actions will take two or more years to implement (as they often do), don't expect major performance improvements within the first nine months.

Military historians tell us that wars are won battle by battle, even skirmish by skirmish. The troops need to go through the experience of developing the confidence that they can win.

To do so, they have to regroup both during and after battles, reexamine the map of the battlefield, and agree on a new strategy for the next offensive.

TIP▶ Showcase Your Success

Some of the most action-responsive companies we interviewed demonstrate the capacity to manage action at a breathtaking pace on a number of fronts. They do so without the signs of fatigue we saw in less responsive companies engaged in longer-term projects.

So what's our point? Just this: Managers of long-term actions must present measurable achievements at strategic moments.

Some companies have showcased a successful business unit, area, or group of workers who have broken through a barrier and achieved an impressive result. Everyone can be energized by a reminder of the successes that a project has achieved so far.

TIP▶ Bring the Vision to Everyone

All employees must recognize that they have a stake in the success or failure of the action and that they own a piece of it. If you do not spend time ensuring that team members fully understand how your vision will work in practice, then you run the risk of action fatigue.

▶ _____

LEARN BY EXAMPLE: **Ricoh**

When Ricoh, the Japanese manufacturer of copiers, instructed its French subsidiary to double sales over a four-year period in order to become the number-two player in the French market, the required reengineering exercise seemed relatively straightforward.

But in practice, the action turned out to be much more complicated. Initially, marketing and sales strategies were evaluated and redesigned to achieve the desired increase in growth. However, the subsidiary still held onto restrictive sales policies instituted when it had been a Ricoh distributor. These policies were at odds with the role of a subsidiary company.

In addition, managers at the Paris headquarters had to referee disputes between regional sales forces and dealers. Customer service, a victim of the not-invented-here syndrome, suffered immeasurably.

Ricoh attacked the problems by reengineering six top-level business processes. A substantial restructuring of the sales force and distribution channel supported the reengineering. A series of 27 clearly defined subprojects was constructed, phased in over a period of months. Phased implementation, it was hoped, would allow employees to take on the changes with less disruption to sales performance.

The action was launched as part of an annual meeting of 350 managers and senior salespeople. The vision and implementation preparation, however, proved insufficiently detailed. "We relied too much on local managers to interpret and communicate the details locally," says subsidiary president Bernard Decugis. "We should have spent more time understanding exactly how job descriptions were going to change, how people were going to work differently—person by person."

However intense the work and dedicated the salespeople, performance began to drop as implementation proceeded. The later phasing of the information system aggravated the problem. "Existing local systems had to be used in conjunction with new ways of working," explains Decugis. Ricoh launched a special bonus scheme to drive up performance during the transition period.

By the end of the first year, sales volume growth had slowed to just 6 percent. "We needed a full year to digest the transition and the inevitable turbulence of the changes," reflects Decugis.

By the conclusion of the second financial year (1977), Decugis is proud to report, "Our performance improved dramatically to 37 percent sales volume growth. We achieved our targets of number-two ranking in the French market and doubling of sales volume growth one year ahead of plan."

Ricoh's experience graphically illustrates the challenges of explaining exactly how a vision will work in practice and maintaining performance during transition.

Action Paths

Here's our advice on combating action fatigue for each action path.

►Action Path Sprint

Set—and keep—stretch goals.

Establish precise monitoring systems to assess progress weekly.

►Action Path High Jump

Use tracking to keep everyone aware of how you are doing *today.*

Prepare for organizational recovery by gathering stakeholders to discuss personal issues.

Manage dips in morale—different groups will experience lulls at different times.

►Action Path Decathlon

Anticipate action-team fatigue, as well as pessimism about promised benefits, if past actions have been unsuccessful.

Curb defections to "new and improved" solutions before the benefits of your action have been achieved.

▶ACTION PATH   **Marathon**

Keep the action team fresh by turning over some members at the midpoint.

Assure that the final phase doesn't run out of steam.

Build changing measures into the action-assessment system.

Questions and Answers

QUESTION: Is fatigue inevitable?

Unfortunately, the answer is yes. Fatigue strikes long-term and short-term actions alike. But, we should warn you, long-term actions—meaning marathons and decathlons—are especially vulnerable.

Our rule: *The longer an action lasts, the more likely it is that fatigue will stop it in its tracks.*

QUESTION: Does fatigue strike everyone?

Our experience shows that it does, hitting the action team first, then spreading throughout the organization.

QUESTION: How else can I build support for my action?

Pilot programs are a good way to build support and ownership. Piloting in a single area or a whole business unit will, if successful, help inspire organizationwide confidence in the action.

As noted in previous chapters, Bristol-Myers Squibb and other companies have created pilot programs that allow employees to get a vision of the organization's future operations.

Moreover, a pilot enables the action team to take preventative measures and thus limits having to struggle to energize at a later date.

QUESTION: My action program has lasted two years—do I have to keep my employees up to speed on every detail?

Keeping the workforce informed with regular interactive communication helps maintain effort and morale—and helps combat fatigue. Consequently, the company stays energized, and the action project stays on track.

At Bank Corporation, Daniel Wright is convinced that open communication played a pivotal role in his project's climb back up the action curve:

> As soon as we started announcing things, telling people facts about the future, you could see morale starting to swing back.
>
> A fear of the unknown is what drives down morale. When things are known, then a decision can be made. The employee thinks, "If I don't like it, I can react to it." So that helps morale.

Motivation increases when employees get enough time for relaxation. Anything that aids in conserving energy will help in the long run.

QUESTION: When do I give my people a break?

When it comes to understanding that harried workers need a break, Delores Marciel at Adaptec is more savvy than most. At a juncture that she termed "absolute crunch time" in the Apex program, Marciel loaded her team onto a bus and took them to the aquarium for the day:

> The idea is that they are all stressed, so we are going to go play for a few hours. It has to be done. So tomorrow morning, a bus is going to roll up outside with beer and wine and snacks. We are going to

spend two hours driving, we are going to have lunch at a restaurant, we are going to walk around and not talk about work.

Frederick Bräutigan, project director of the logistics department at Siemens Medical, advises:

To be successful, build on success. Show your successes! If you have done a good job, just talk about it.

In a word, *celebrate!*

LIFE IS ACTION

Managing action is a process of reconceiving, rearranging, and retooling old ways. It affects systems, structures, and processes. It also affects people, including action managers. Euphoria, frustration, elation, disappointment—all those emotions and more surface during an action. Why? Because it's life.

13

ACTION MANAGERS IN ACTION

*We have looked at the key challenges of managing action
and have suggested practical responses. Now,
let's look at what it means to you.*

Step by step, we've gone through the issues and situations that, we believe, harbor the potential for knocking action onto the fast track:

How to plan

How to help your leaders lead

How to allocate your resources

We've told you about communication, people, processes, technology, and more—all in an effort to give you the best shot at achieving the goals envisioned for your action.

Through it all, the spotlight has been on what you, Mr. or Ms. Action Manager, must do to stay in the race.

But while we have primed you to meet the challenges that will confront your program, scant attention has been paid to the challenges that will confront you personally as you carry out your monumental task.

Putting a more personal face on the whole concept of action management, we now turn the discussion to what you can expect your life and career to be like when you choose to take on the role of action manager.

Drawing on the actual experiences and feelings of real-world action managers with whom we have worked, we can give you an idea of the exhilaration and exhaustion, the stresses and the satisfactions, the gut-wrenching decisions and the spirit-lifting accomplishments that await you.

Our panel of experts offers insights and hard-won lessons from the trenches that help to illuminate the reality of action management, for better or worse.

Listen to what our interviewees have to say about the life-changing experience of managing a major business action. Although all names have been changed, the experiences they recount are very real indeed.

Herewith, a roundup of comments from five savvy, action-tested managers.

"If I took all of those people, the company was going to crash."

Herb, of Katya Systems, Inc., was attending an offsite leadership seminar when he was summoned to the chief operating officer's suite to learn that he had been selected to lead a major business process reengineering effort to install an enterprise resource planning (ERP) system.

Given only a couple of hours to mull it over, Herb accepted, the announcement was made the following morning, and he had to hit the ground running.

> HERB: The biggest challenge I faced all at once was how to put together a team of folks. First, I had to figure out what it was I was expected to do, and then I had to decide what team I needed to put together to be a winner.
>
> I couldn't have as full-time members the director and vice-president-level folks who were running the procurement department, the planning department, the finance department, and the controller.

If I took all of those people, the company was going to crash. We were trying to grow at 35 percent that particular year, and these people were straining at the seams just trying to hold it together.

On the other hand, if I didn't have those people locked in, then I was hosed, because they controlled all the resources, both people and money.

I ended up convincing them that they had to give me a really good person from their organizations and that person had to be full-time. They wanted to give me the dregs, the people they wanted to fire but didn't have the guts to, so I had to fight through that. It took a lot of one-on-one conversations where my relationships with the process owners, who were the vice presidents and directors, were worked out.

Herb readily admits that his new role thrust him into a totally unfamiliar environment. He turned to outside facilitators to smooth the transition.

HERB: Twenty-five years in engineering didn't prepare me to do *re*engineering. My engineering knowledge per se was virtually useless. As it turned out, my program- and project-management skills, my people skills, the relationships I'd built, my organized way of thinking, my project-scheduling capabilities—all of those turned out to be my salvation as we went through the project.

One problem I had was understanding that the folks that I was working with were driven by a completely different set of motivations than those I was familiar with.

Engineers primarily are motivated by the challenge of the project—that they get to do something with new technology. The procurement, finance, and materials people—they were primarily motivated by how this worked into their career paths. And all of the fringes (salary increases, bonuses) were important to them. That was an interesting learning experience for me.

I actually had two outside executive coaches that I used about one hour a month each. I would talk to them about the people problems I was having, ask them what I could do to fix things. Those two were instrumental in helping me out. They were able to keep me on track.

Herb was generally very positive about his treatment by colleagues during the action program, although one issue did provoke animosity among his peers.

Katya Systems traditionally posts flat second-quarter revenues, because the lengthy vacation schedules that are common throughout Europe cut into its overseas results. In anticipation of this cyclical downturn, Katya freezes hiring. But because of the nature of the action program, Herb was allowed to continue hiring, and this raised some hackles. He wisely chose to meet the negativism head-on.

> HERB: There was a tremendous amount of bitterness from the other members, asking, "Well, how come Herb gets to hire and we're cut off?" That was probably one of the more difficult things to get past.
>
> If I had allowed that passive resistance to get in place, it would have killed the project. So I went up in front of the entire company at an all-employee meeting and explained to them what we were doing and why with respect to the hiring. Although they didn't like it, they weren't going to actively fight it.

Dissension of another, ultimately more serious, kind flared when Herb brought the process owners together to discuss what he perceived as the three interconnected parts of the project: automation, process, and organization.

> HERB: When I laid out a straw organization, two of the vice-president-, director-level people leapt out of their chairs and said, "If you touch my organization, I quit!" After the meeting, others told me the same thing.
>
> I found out all of a sudden that 80 percent of my process-owner-level staff was going to quit if we made organizational changes. The

executive steering committee and the CEO basically felt the same way: "Don't touch the organization. End of message."

Having to give up 25 percent of the efficiencies that we could have obtained was personally very devastating for me. In retrospect, I would get agreement early on with respect to what can be changed. Not being allowed to touch the organization kept me from delivering on part of my expectations.

"Without the leadership to reinforce that what we were doing was important, I had to find it from within."

Phoebe, who works for World King Entertainment Company, was in the middle of an ERP implementation when her department was merged with another business unit. The team opted to continue the implementation, without including the new entity.

Phoebe told us about an unusual series of events that might well have sunk any other such project, including three different chief financial officers during the nine-month first phase of the implementation, a change in the partner on the project, and changes in the leadership of the information-systems department.

> PHOEBE: We suffered from a classic case of not having strong executive sponsorship due to three CFO changes during the project. Just to build somebody's confidence in the project takes longer than eight or nine months, and having to do that three times didn't set us up for success.
>
> Without the leadership to reinforce that what we were doing was important, I had to find it from within. That was not optimal. No matter how strong you are, you always need someone above you to agree that the priority is the right priority.
>
> With all the noise being created above us, part of my job became to shelter and shield the team. We just had to keep going to get it done, and done on time and on budget, and I had to keep moving the forces forward regardless of what was going on.

As times get tough, you tend to be more insular. Now I realize that that was when we really needed to communicate more and pull users in more. We didn't do that.

I have learned that someone has to stay above it and not be so much into the details. They need to focus on the external stakeholders. That is key to success.

This time it is very clear. We have a strong stakeholder group. We meet with them on a regular basis. I have shifted my time more toward managing the stakeholders. I am more focused on working the leadership level, so when I hear comments, I get the right person on the team to go partner with them.

Saying that the professional and personal were intertwined, Phoebe expanded on what her life was like during the action.

PHOEBE: Neither I nor the person I reported to had any idea how much time this would take. It was one of a number of things I was doing, but the ideal way to do it is full time.

When you are going through an ERP system implementation, the last 6 months of it are a 24-hour-a-day, 7-day-a-week-type job. Having people doing testing or whatever, many of whom didn't have a direct boss, I felt somewhat responsible for their coaching, mentoring, nurturing, keeping their spirits up, and so on.

This meant getting phone calls in the middle of the night. There were faxes and beeps at very odd hours. Sometimes it was because they were getting frustrated and were hitting the wall. I didn't have the technical knowledge to help them, but I could be there to support them.

When the project becomes all encompassing, the separation of your personal and professional life isn't clear.

Phoebe had specific suggestions as to what someone who is embarking on this kind of large-scale project should do to prepare.

PHOEBE: Clear your plate of other projects as much as you can. Spend some time getting to know the folks on your team—learn their strengths and weaknesses.

In the early stages of your team's formulation, pay attention to any pink flags—meaning not quite the red flag—that go up with respect to anyone on the team. It could be something in the back of your mind indicating that there is not quite a fit.

If you have these doubts more than a couple of times, you are probably better off making a change in the team composition sooner rather than later—99 percent of the time, you will be right.

Also, make sure that you personally are educated as much as you can be from the outside, looking at projects similar to the one you are about to embark on. Find out what has been a success and, more important, what has failed and why it failed. Focus on the things not to do.

In addition, fight for yourself. Don't leave it to chance. These projects are never easy. They are never risk-free. Lay out clearly what the end game is for yourself.

Keep the communication flowing. When you hit tough times, balance the need to shield the team with the need to communicate to your leaders what is going wrong. You don't want a catastrophe to be the first signal that something is going wrong.

Phoebe readily admits that issues of action scope and limits are immense, and says that they must be very clearly defined.

PHOEBE: Probably one of the most challenging things is to put a scope around [action]—to define what the boundaries are.

I compare it to remodeling a house. You set out to do a certain job, and, as you see the progress and the improvement, the next room doesn't look as good and so on. It's pretty easy to start off small and, before you know it, you have doubled and tripled it. You have to stay focused on what the end game is and realize that breaking into phases is probably a better way to go.

Professionally, you have to show some wins along the way, so by breaking it into smaller mountains and conquering them one at a time, you can demonstrate progress and keep the leadership of the organization excited about the project, too. Then, you can always answer the question, "So what have you done for me lately?"

Family relationships can easily suffer during an intense and time-consuming action.

PHOEBE: Have heart-to-heart discussions in the household about specific things like child care, who comes home at what time, and when you need extra freedom. You really need support on the home front.

In a leadership role, you want to be an enabler, not an obstacle. In a risky situation, you are probably going to want to review and control things even more, and you will need rapid turnaround time to keep the staff productive. That will eat into greater amounts of your personal time. Frequently, I get a fax at 10:00 P.M. and have to fax my responses back so that the answers are there for people who came in early the next morning.

Just as you can't overcommunicate on a project, you need to do the same on the home front. You need to remind them of the project schedule. It is almost like treating your personal important people as key stakeholders.

Phoebe told us how this experience has changed her career.

PHOEBE: It has made me more marketable on the outside. There aren't too many people who have gone through two [ERP implementations].

Inside the company, it has made me more of a resource as other business units install ERP systems. They seek out advice and counsel, which gives me the opportunity to make certain relationships even stronger, because I am working in an advisory role.

Among my peers, I am recognized as a resource or a knowledge base for them.

"The paradoxes will kill you."

Tim, of Anja Filmworks Ltd., views the career impact of managing a major action in a somewhat different light, and sees a definite distinction between program management and project management.

> TIM: One of the big benefits of doing this work is that it is management training, and you can apply that anywhere. If you come into this job with experience in some business, this job will add to your management skills. So you should be able to go back into that business at a higher level.
>
> But I don't think it is going to automatically give you opportunities outside whatever previous business experience you had. This is really non-business-specific work.
>
> Every time we do a project in any given area, I learn about that area of business—but I don't become an expert in that area. People are not going to hire me in marketing just because I happen to manage a marketing reengineering project. I have not done marketing. What I have done is manage the process.

Tim also offers some specific requirements for taking on this type of work.

> TIM: The requirements are perseverance, tenacity, having thick skin, having a thorough understanding of the business, and being very diplomatic. This is in addition to the management skills you have to bring to the table.
>
> All of this is essential if you are going to overcome what I see as a series of critical paradoxes. It is the paradoxes that will kill you.

One example is that you have to be diplomatic and sensitive to the political environment, yet you have to get tough when people resist. This is a difficult challenge to meet.

Another example is that you have to improve performance, yet you can't disrupt the business. You also have to be able to establish good working relationships with higher-level executives who normally wouldn't want to associate with you. They usually don't want you present.

The next thing is that you have to be responsible for managing [an action] effort over which you have virtually no control. You have to personally drive the effort, but you have to make sure that the right people take all the responsibility and get all the credit.

Last, from my perspective, is that you have to be able to succeed when most projects around the world fail.

Tim has been involved in a major reengineering effort at Anya Filmworks that is being implemented in incremental pieces. The program has sought to use its increasing capabilities, capacity, reputation, and successes as leverage to move into large operational actions.

TIM: I feel a tremendous sense of satisfaction at having built a team of people internally who are going out and doing projects now, and who are much less dependent on help. Our reputation is quite good.

Then there is the exposure. In playing this role, you almost always have a lot of meetings with top, senior-level executives of the company. They get to know who you are. That can be a positive thing or a negative thing.

It can be tough when you are above the radar line. People know you. They know about what is good and what is bad. It is very challenging. But the exposure I think is generally a positive thing.

Next is experience. You can't pay to get the kind of experience this type of work brings you . . . to manage this many projects, with such a high profile, this many people, to work with the executives, and to learn about the various different areas of the business. You can't pay for that. It's invaluable.

And there is the knowledge itself. You learn so much, not just about the business but about change, people, psychology, and analytical techniques.

Tim is quick to point out, however, that all is not sunshine and roses in a major action program.

> TIM: On the negative side, the primary effect is exhaustion. This is really hard work.
>
> It is very challenging mentally to overcome the paradoxes every day. It is challenging to deal with the resistance, the problems, and managing people's expectations. It is very wearing. The more projects you have going, the more external consultants you have in-house, the more challenging it becomes.
>
> Then there is the Darth Vader syndrome. . . . You have complicated projects and you have to make some changes to executive management. You have to be tough occasionally, and pretty soon, you turn into that dark, lurking figure image. People are afraid when they see you coming down the hallway. They aren't so much resistant anymore, they just have fear.

Asked about his most difficult experiences during the entire action process, Tim mentioned two.

> TIM: I am not sure which one is the hardest, but one was managing external consultants. That is very difficult. They are bigger than you are. They have more control than you do. At the beginning, they know more than you do.
>
> It is very challenging to manage them, still keep costs reasonable, and get the kind of work done that you need before you have a team that can do the work internally.

On the personal side, the hardest thing for me was taking abuse from executives. People behave badly in adversity or any kind of stress. A lot of times they lash out at the nearest and lowest-level person they can find. That is when you have to put the thick skin on.

When asked if he would still sign on to head a major action, Tim had a one-word response: "Definitely."

"You have to keep your own report card."

Austin, who is with Richmore Outfitters, expresses tremendous satisfaction with the results of his company's reengineering program, but there are a few things he would have done differently.

AUSTIN: I probably would have put the internal team in place sooner. We had started the culture change in the organization sooner than we gave ourselves credit for, and we could have just installed that department and moved on more quickly. Besides saving on consulting fees, there is the benefit of having it become part of the culture sooner.

But you also have to be very careful to make sure you've got the right person. If you're going from a situation like we were in, with no exposure to reengineering to saying we want to get this in culture, you can get into big trouble if you don't have the right person to continue it.

As for the future, Austin offers a word of caution.

AUSTIN: People can lose sight of what some of the benefits are after working so hard and so long on a project. Unfortunately, you have to keep your own report card, and be able to periodically remind the organization that here's what [the program is achieving]. And we can point to it.

Don't give up on the report card too soon. A lot of effort goes into these. You want to be able to look back in a couple of years and say what really came out.

I think that some of the challenges I'm going to have are ongoing. [The program] was very high profile for the first couple of years and we had a lot going on. I was reporting to [the top leadership] every three months on the results.

It's part of the culture now. That's the good news. The bad news is it's part of the culture and it's not as high-profile on an individual basis. So we're going to have to keep that up and make periodic reports so people understand what is going on.

"You are going to be exposed to some things that will give you gray hair."

Jeremy, of Sophiebuilt Products International, who co-led a multifunctional team that installed ERP, human-resources, and payroll information systems at his company, speaks with genuine enthusiasm about the positive impact of managing an action while maintaining a healthy sense of pragmatism about the pitfalls.

JEREMY: This will grow you like you have never grown before. A large-scale program will get you to think in ways that you probably never thought of before. It will force you to try to cover more bases than ever before.

If you are not someone who knows anything about the theories, you will get to learn them and see them in action. If you are doing this right, you will get to work with higher levels of management and influence the way businesses are going.

It can be a power trip or it can be real satisfying, depending on your perspective.

It will expose you to the good, the bad, and the ugly parts of the business. You will turn over rocks underneath which all kinds of scorpions are crawling, mainly around policies, practices, and behaviors. You end up having to protect yourself a lot.

Noting that these programs couple high visibility and enormous opportunity with a great deal of risk, Jeremy stresses the need for good sponsorship and commitment, lest "you go down in flames."

> JEREMY: I had to cultivate relationships with the staff. I insisted on regular meetings where we would come in with an issue that needed to be tackled or a position already taken that needed to be approved.
>
> A lot of positioning work had to be done. It just means lobbying. That is the reality of life. These jobs tend to be somewhat political in nature because you are dealing with people's comfort zones and their turfs, established practices that they have had for many years.

Particularly troubling to Jeremy were the realities of team leadership at Sophiebuilt.

> JEREMY: What was frustrating as a leader of the team was that a lot of times it was *my* work and not the team's work.
>
> In a leadership role, you want to promote your team and get them visibility. You want them to get the awards and fruits of their labor. Sometimes, because you are out in front, you are the one that gets a lot of that visibility.
>
> The team leader can fight hard for accolades and applause for the people who work with him, but it doesn't always happen. I was stymied. Some of the bonus stuff that we tried to put in place and some that we had in place, I could control only part of it.
>
> I think the lesson here is that I didn't own the whole project.

As Jeremy discovered, personal relationships can take a beating amid the intensity and pace demanded by an action program. Married only a year when he took the job, Jeremy admits that he had to sacrifice a few things.

JEREMY: From a relationship standpoint, there were some stressers. Initially, I was away from home four to five days a week, living in an apartment in Chicago, and flying home on Thursday nights. I spent a lot of time on airplanes. It was also hard on friendships. I lost a couple of friendships in the process because of lack of contact.

In Chicago, I spent a lot of time working, because there is no one to go home to when you are in an apartment. Twelve- to fourteen-hour days were not uncommon. I didn't go hang out with a lot of people. It was kind of lonely.

Not all of the stresses were personal, of course.

JEREMY: There was a lot of internal stress over some of the high-profile types of people I was meeting. I had to explain to the head of a software maker, for example, why we didn't pick his package.

My information-systems copartner and I had to make a presentation before the rest of the corporation as to why we selected the ERP package. It was exciting, but it was pretty nerve-wracking for someone who was 32 years old at the time.

There is an incredible personal satisfaction that comes from doing these things if you like to do it. You are going to be exposed to some things that will give you gray hair, which I have. You are going to be exposed to some things that will make you hair fall out, which is happening to me, too. But I don't think I would trade it.

Despite the difficulties, one can get addicted to the adrenaline rush that accompanies significant and highly visible accomplishments. The transition back to a more traditional role can be difficult, as well.

JEREMY: It was fast-paced, long days. It was very exciting. It was very busy. I always had the feeling that there was something else to do. I had a team of 100 people. Cutting back a little bit has been hard.

Despite his basic love for the job, Jeremy perceived a risk that he didn't wish to take.

JEREMY: When you are a change agent here, I think you get typecast in the slot that you are in. My hardest decision was sitting down with [my supervisors] and saying that, although I did want to go in and put in the training piece, and the succession-planning piece, and the recruitment piece, if I did this much longer, that is all anyone would see when they looked at me. I didn't want to run that risk.

Jeremy adds a final note of caution.

JEREMY: You get caught up in the emotion and the zeal—the juices that are flowing in your team. That is a good thing.

The difficulty lies in the fact that you may spill that eagerness, zeal, and excitement into your client community. If they catch that enthusiasm and you don't put some parameters and brakes on it, their expectations will be at such a high level that what you deliver will never meet their needs. People end up saying, "What happened was what you said it was, but it wasn't what I was expecting."

That was frustrating and demotivating for me and some of the team. You have to bring expectations down by consistently painting the right picture for people and reinforcing that message over and over again.

On the personal side, you get so passionate about the project that you have this huge sense of letdown when you don't deliver on that or when people override your expectations.

EPILOGUE

We believe business is a race. We believe business is action. Indeed, we believe life is action and action is life.

Managing action challenges you to recalibrate your way of thinking and take into account the fact that every company goes through its own stages of the business race. Each encounters new competitive pressures, new global realities, and new customer demands.

To remain healthy as the race progresses, a business must respond by taking the appropriate action. Perhaps it reengineers processes, restructures operations, even merges with or acquires other companies.

Sometimes, in its quest to take whatever action is needed to maintain good health, an organization might take a nasty spill as it trips over unforeseen bumps along the course. These bumps may arise from a lack of proper planning, a need for smart leadership, or a failure to gather adequate resources. Or, maybe, the stumbling block takes its shape from a company's ill-conceived, or even nonexistent, effort to communicate pertinent needs and ideas.

In the preceding chapters, we have shined the light of foreknowledge on the bumps as we discussed the 10 challenges—plan, allocate, lead, strengthen, mobilize, clarify, cultivate, integrate, wire, and reenergize—that every action manager must confront. And we have offered suggestions and techniques gleaned from our own years of experience to help you sidestep the danger spots that dot your path.

Although much of our discussion has necessarily centered around the organization as a whole, we know, of course, that the whole is made up of many parts—the most important being the people. So to effectively illustrate the ways in which action impacts on people, both personally and professionally, we have made you privy to the real words of real action managers. We have shared the case histories of real companies that lived and prospered through their own major actions.

Armed with the understanding that can come only from such practical exposure to both the triumphs and the missteps of others, it is our hope that you have gained a sense of what lies ahead for you and your company in today's complex business environment—an environment that demands nearly continuous action just to stay in the race. Whatever pitfalls you encounter as you make your way around the business track, we encourage you to use the lessons found in these pages to help maintain your footing and guide your business safely across the finish line.

ACKNOWLEDGMENTS

How to decide who to acknowledge for their influence on a book that arises out of the vast arena of consulting and line-management experience is not a easy task. This book reflects the experience accumulated from the trials and tribulations of thousands of clients and consultants. Above all else we thank all of them for their indirect input to this book.

More specifically, we pay tribute to the huge effort that our friend and colleague Graham Perrott put into helping us to develop the content and structure of this book.

We could not have written a how-to book of any consequence without real-life examples on which to base our observations and advice, so we are grateful to all of those organizations that participated in our PwC / MORI Global Action Survey on an anonymous basis. In addition, many companies were sufficiently generous with their time and impressively open enough about their experiences to provide us with deep and insightful information about their own experiences of running actions. We thank them for being patient with the long gestation of this book and for their support.

In a global firm of 140,000 staff we would be foolish to ignore the huge opportunities for help which are available on a task of this nature. We took full advantage of this, and particularly helpful in their contribution of ideas and information were Geoff Dodds, Peter Davis, Colin Price, Matt English, David Tunney, Dexter Hendrix, Frederick Miller, Jeremy Wilkes, Lester-Gabis Levine, Maggie Lucas, Marina Capaccini, Ralph Baines, Ruth McLenaghan, and Simon Young.

In addition, we are grateful for the inputs and time given by Adrian Edwards, Albert Mauritius, Andy Embury, Jane Lucien-Schole, Breda Robertson, Celeste Coruzzi, David Dickinson, Debbie Cohen, Denis

Collart, Dick Watkin, Gerry Miles, Gonzalo Suarez, Greg Meyding, Ian Beesley, Joe Marino, Marilyn Stemper, Matt Porta, Mike Tierney, Nikki Ross, Peter Barlow, Richard Lucas, Robert Brown, Sandra Rickner, Sara Markley, Scott Feder, Scott Kaufman, Stephen Bradley, Steve Brown, Susan Blum, Tom Dougherty, Uwe Mueller, Chris White, Nicola Adamson, Doug Kramer, Maryline Damour, and Lubna Azhar.

The guidance and advice of Donna Carpenter and her colleagues at WordWorks were critical to the realization of this book. Mo Coyle was exceptional in his ability to hold the threads together and guide us on questions of structure. Martha Lawler kept the whole thing together with supreme patience. Ruth Hlavacek, Susanna Ketchum, and Pat Wright were dedicated contributors. Our agent Helen Rees has been a source of energy and good humor throughout and has ensured that we actually got the book to press.

Richard Pascale has been a good friend to PwC and has honored us with his ideas and insights both through his own books and in classes run with our partners. We are grateful for his introduction to our book.

Finally and most important, we want to thank our families. Writing a book is never a project for the normal working day and it has been a demanding task as much for them as it has for us. To our wives, Gabriele, Laura, and Cathy, and our children, Katya, Anja, Sophie, Phoebe, Max, Sam, Leanna Rose, and Christina: Thank you.

INDEX